R O M A N
MYTHOLOGY

*A Collection of the
Best Roman Myths*

JASON DODD

TABLE OF CONTENTS

INTRODUCTION

In the pantheon of world mythologies, Roman mythology holds a place of distinction, offering a rich tapestry of stories that have captivated the imagination for centuries. "Roman Mythology: A Collection of the Best Roman Myths" is a journey into the heart of ancient Rome, exploring its gods and goddesses, legendary heroes, and foundational myths. This collection serves not only as a window into the ancient Roman worldview but also as a mirror reflecting the timeless human quest for meaning, understanding, and inspiration.

In the opening chapter, we delve into the world of the Roman gods and goddesses. These deities, from the mighty Jupiter, king of the gods, to the nurturing Venus, goddess of love and beauty, are the cornerstone of Roman mythological tradition. Their stories, lineage, and influence weave a complex hierarchy that echoes the societal and moral values of ancient Rome. This chapter serves as a guide to understanding the roles and relationships of these divine beings and their significance in the larger narrative of Roman mythology.

Chapter 2 expands our exploration to include a diverse cast of characters that enrich Roman myths: demi-gods, heroes, mortals, nymphs, monsters, and more. These figures often bridge the world of the divine and the mortal, bringing the extraordinary into the realm of the everyday. Their tales are filled with adventure, conflict, and lessons that resonate through time.

The narrative continues in Chapter 3 with the Roman Creation Myth, delving into the ancient Roman understanding of the universe's origins. This chapter explores how the Romans envisioned the creation of the world and the forces at play in this primordial saga, offering insights into their cosmological beliefs.

Chapter 4 recounts one of the most pivotal stories in Roman mythology: the founding of Rome by Romulus and Remus. This tale is not just a story of a city's physical birth but also a narrative about the ideals, struggles, and aspirations that would define Roman identity.

In Chapter 5, we explore the dramatic and complex story of the Rape of the Sabine Women. This myth, involving themes of conflict, integration, and reconciliation, offers a profound look at the early societal structure of Rome and its surrounding regions.

The Calydonian Boar Hunt, recounted in Chapter 6, is a thrilling tale of heroism and adventure, highlighting the valor and prowess of Roman heroes while intertwining themes of human and divine interactions.

Chapter 7 brings us the enchanting story of Vertumnus and Pomona, a narrative that celebrates the gentler aspects of Roman mythology, focusing on themes of love, transformation, and persuasion.

In Chapter 8, we delve into the story of Hercules and Cacus, a myth that exemplifies the intersection of heroism and moral complexities, set against the backdrop of what would become one of the greatest cities in history.

Finally, Chapter 9 concludes our collection with the tale of Jupiter and the Bee, a fable that encapsulates the wisdom of humility and the consequences of overreaching ambition.

"Roman Mythology: A Collection of the Best Roman Myths" invites readers on a journey through the stories that shaped Roman culture and continue to influence our world today. Through these myths, we explore not just the beliefs of an ancient civilization but also the enduring human questions about fate, virtue, and the nature of the divine. Welcome to a world where gods walk among mortals, where heroes battle monsters, and where the tales of old still whisper truths for the modern ear.

CHAPTER 1:
GODS & GODDESSES

Roman mythology is home to a wide array of Gods & Goddesses, each with their own unique role and characteristics in the mythology. In this chapter, we will introduce you to these many fascinating deities. If you are familiar with Greek mythology, you may notice some striking similarities between its pantheon and the deities discussed here.

In Roman mythology, we encounter a pantheon where many gods bear striking resemblances to their Greek counterparts, a reflection of the deep cultural and historical interplay between Rome and ancient Greece. This phenomenon, rooted in the Romans' practice of interpretatio graeca, saw Roman deities merging with Greek gods, adopting their attributes and narratives. This synthesis, however, was not a mere replication.

Roman gods, while similar, were adapted to fit the unique contours of Roman society and values. For instance, Mars, akin to the Greek Ares in being a god of war, was also revered as a guardian of Rome and a symbol of Roman military virtue, aspects less prominent in Ares' Greek narrative. Likewise,

Venus, parallel to the Greek Aphrodite, gained a broader civic and maternal significance in Rome, transcending her Greek origins as primarily a goddess of love and beauty. These adaptations highlight a key facet of Roman mythology: its ability to absorb and recontextualize the divine, creating deities that resonated with Roman identity and societal ethos.

Without further ado, let's dive into the Roman pantheon!

The Primordial Deities

Saturn

Saturn in Roman mythology is a revered and ancient deity, emblematic of the agricultural foundation of Roman culture. As the god of agriculture, wealth, liberation, and time, Saturn's influence is deeply woven into the fabric of Roman society. His reign is mythologically associated with the Golden Age, a period marked by peace, prosperity, and an absence of social hierarchy or labor. This era represented an ideal state of natural abundance and harmony, where the earth freely offered its bounty to humankind.

Saturn's significance in Roman culture is most vividly celebrated during the Saturnalia, a festival held in December. This festivity was a time of joy and liberation, characterized by role reversals, feasting, and a general suspension of societal norms, symbolizing the freedom and equality of the Golden Age. The Temple of Saturn in the Roman Forum, which also served as the state treasury, underscores his role as a bringer of abundance and prosperity.

Unlike other deities who might symbolize more abstract concepts, Saturn's imagery and attributes, such as the sickle, directly connect him with the practical and vital aspects of agriculture – sowing, cultivation, and harvest. His portrayal as a benevolent and generous god reflects the Romans' deep appreciation for the earth's fertility and its critical role in sustaining life and society. Saturn, therefore, occupies a unique and revered position in Roman mythology, representing not just the cycles of time but also the foundational values and sustenance of Roman civilization itself.

Janus

In Roman mythology, Janus stands as a uniquely Roman deity with no direct parallel in other ancient mythologies. He is the god of beginnings, transitions, time, duality, doorways, passages, and endings, making him one of the most important and complex gods in the Roman pantheon. Janus is typically depicted with two faces, looking both forward and backward, symbolizing his ability to see into both the past and the future. This dual aspect made him a god of transitions, presiding over every kind of beginning, whether abstract or concrete, from the birth of a child to the start of a new enterprise or the change of seasons.

Janus' significance in Roman religion is evident in the fact that he was often invoked first in prayers, regardless of the main deity being worshipped, signifying his role as the opener of the way. The month of January, the beginning of the new year, is named after him, further underscoring his association with beginnings and transitions.

In myth, Janus held a unique position as one of the earliest kings of Latium or even Rome itself, often credited with bringing civilization to the Latins, including the introduction of coinage, laws, and agriculture. The Gates of Janus in the Roman Forum, which were opened in times of war and closed during peace, signify his role as a protector and a symbol of peace and war. His two faces looking in opposite directions also metaphorically represented the peace and war dichotomy, indicating his role in the transitions between these two states. Janus, thus, embodies the essence of change and transition, playing a pivotal role in Roman culture and religious practices.

Ops

In Roman mythology, Ops is a significant goddess embodying the earth's fertility and abundance. Her name, meaning "wealth" or "abundance," reflects her role as a deity of agricultural bounty and resourcefulness. Ops is regarded as the consort of Saturn, the god of agriculture and time, and together they are often associated with the prosperity of the Golden Age, a time of plenty and peace.

Ops holds a central place in the Roman agricultural calendar, with festivals such as Opiconsivia and Opalia celebrated in her honor. These festivals were crucial for invoking her blessings for a bountiful harvest and overall prosperity. Her worship was deeply intertwined with the well-being of the Roman state and its people, emphasizing the importance of agriculture in sustaining the community and ensuring its prosperity.

As a motherly figure, Ops also represents the nurturing aspect of the earth, providing sustenance and support to all life. She was revered as a protective goddess, ensuring the fertility of the land and the well-being of the people who depend on it. In religious iconography, she is sometimes depicted in a manner that highlights her generous and bountiful nature, often shown with a cornucopia, the symbol of abundance and prosperity.

Ops' role extends beyond mere agricultural fertility, symbolizing the broader concept of abundance, both material and spiritual. Her presence in Roman mythology underscores the deep connection the Romans felt with the land and its cycles, reflecting their appreciation and respect for the earth's natural resources and the need for harmony with the natural world.

Caelus

Caelus in Roman mythology is the primordial god of the sky, embodying the celestial expanse and its vastness. As one of the ancient Roman deities, Caelus represents the limitless sky above, a fundamental aspect of the world as understood by the Romans. His role in Roman mythology is deeply connected to the creation and structure of the cosmos, where he is often seen as the heavenly counterpart to Terra, the earth goddess.

While Caelus is not as prominent in myths and religious practices as some other Roman deities, his presence is pivotal in the early Roman creation narratives. As the personification of the sky, Caelus was believed to cover the earth, enveloping the world and providing a divine canopy over all existence. This portrayal reflects the Roman understanding of the universe's structure, where the sky was a vast, overarching entity, integral to the fabric of the world.

In Roman religious thought, Caelus was also associated with the divine and the ethereal aspects of existence. His representation of the sky extended to the celestial and the heavenly, symbolizing the abode of the gods and the realm of the divine. As such, Caelus occupied a fundamental place in the Roman worldview, representing the boundless sky's omnipresence and its overarching influence over the earthly realm. His character as a sky deity highlights the Romans' reverence for the natural world and its components, which they saw as imbued with divine significance and power.

Terra

In Roman mythology, Terra, also known as Tellus Mater, is the personification of the Earth and one of the oldest Roman deities. She embodies the solid ground upon which all life exists and is revered as a motherly figure, nurturing and supporting all forms of life. As a primordial goddess, Terra's role extends beyond mere fertility; she is the very essence of the Earth, representing its diverse aspects - from the fertile soil that yields crops to the untamed wilderness.

Terra was worshipped as a vital force of nature, essential for agriculture and sustenance. Her importance in Roman culture is reflected in various festivals and rituals, particularly those related to agriculture and fertility. One such celebration, the Fordicidia, involved sacrifices to ensure the Earth's fertility for the coming planting season. During the Sementivae, a sowing festival, Terra was invoked to bless the seeds and ensure a bountiful harvest.

In Roman art and literature, Terra is often portrayed as a nurturing, motherly figure, sometimes depicted reclining with fruits and grains, symbolizing her role in agriculture and abundance. She is also seen as a more general symbol of nature and the natural world, encompassing all aspects of the Earth's bounty.

Terra's significance in Roman mythology reflects the deep connection and reverence the Romans had for the Earth. As a fundamental deity, she represents not just the physical ground but also the life-giving and sustaining qualities of the Earth, crucial for the survival and prosperity of both individuals and the Roman state as a whole. Her worship underscores the Romans' appreciation of the natural world and their understanding of humanity's dependence on the Earth's resources.

The Dii Consentes

Akin to the 12 Olympians in Greek mythology, the Dii Consentes gods are the 12 primary deities that the Romans recognized and worshipped.

Jupiter

In Roman mythology, Jupiter stands as the supreme deity, ruling over the Roman pantheon as the king of the gods. His dominion extends to the sky and all its phenomena, from the thunderbolt to the weather, embodying the concept of divine authority and sovereignty. Known also as Jove, Jupiter is a god of light and protection, revered as the guardian of Rome and its people, and is often associated with law, social order, and governance.

Jupiter's role in Roman religion and culture is multifaceted. He is seen as the protector of the state, and his temple on the Capitoline Hill, one of the most important and revered sanctuaries in Rome, was a symbol of the city's strength and unity. As the chief deity, Jupiter was often invoked in state ceremonies, oaths, and important public events, underscoring his role as the upholder of law and order. The festival of Jupiter Optimus Maximus, celebrated on September 13th, was one of the most significant in the Roman calendar, marking the dedication of his temple.

In addition to his political and social significance, Jupiter also played a vital role in Roman mythology as a character in various myths and legends, often representing the archetypal figure of power and authority. He is frequently depicted holding a thunderbolt, his most recognized attribute, symbolizing his control over the forces of nature and his role as a divine arbiter.

Jupiter's influence extended beyond the confines of mythology into the daily lives of the Romans. His omnipresence in religious, political, and social spheres made him an integral part of Roman identity, embodying the ideals of Roman leadership, authority, and paternal protection. As such, Jupiter occupied a central place in Roman worship and was considered the most powerful and revered of all the Roman gods.

Juno

In Roman mythology, Juno is a preeminent goddess, revered as the queen of the gods and the divine protector of the Roman state and its women. She is the wife and sister of Jupiter, the king of the gods, and together they form a powerful divine pair. Juno's domains are multifaceted, encompassing aspects of marriage, childbirth, and the female identity, as well as the broader spheres of fertility, protection, and sovereignty.

Juno's significance in Roman society is highlighted by her role as the guardian of the Roman state. She is often depicted in a regal manner, symbolizing her status as the queen of the gods and her association with the Roman Empire's power and authority. Juno is also intimately connected to the welfare and protection of women, particularly in their roles as wives and mothers. Her festival, Matronalia, celebrated on March 1st, was dedicated to her role in marriage and motherhood, where women would offer prayers and gifts to Juno for their wellbeing and that of their families.

Apart from her maternal and marital attributes, Juno also held military associations. She was worshipped as Juno Regina (Juno the Queen) and Juno Sospita (Juno the Savior), reflecting her role as a protectress in times of war and conflict. In these aspects, she was seen as a defender of the Roman people, embodying the strength and resilience of the Roman state.

Juno's temples and cults were among the most significant in Rome, with the Temple of Juno Moneta on the Capitoline Hill serving not only as a religious site but also as the Roman mint, further linking her to the state's prosperity and stability. In all these roles, Juno was deeply woven into the fabric of Roman life, representing the ideal of Roman womanhood and the divine embodiment of the state's protective and nurturing qualities.

Neptune

In Roman mythology, Neptune is a powerful deity, revered as the god of freshwater and the sea. His role extends beyond the mere dominion over waters; he is also associated with horses and, by extension, with earthquakes. Neptune's significance in Roman religion is highlighted by his control over all water bodies, from the vast ocean to the smallest streams, symbolizing the essential and omnipresent nature of water in Roman life and the natural world.

Neptune's worship in Rome was marked by the Neptunalia, a festival celebrated on July 23rd, during the height of summer droughts, to invoke his aid in supplying water and preventing drought. This celebration underscores his importance in agriculture and the survival of the Roman people, as water was crucial for irrigation and sustaining crops.

Although Neptune is often depicted with attributes similar to his portrayal in later cultures, such as holding a trident, his original Roman aspects were more focused on fresh waters and their life-giving properties. His connection with horses, another primary aspect of his worship, is seen in his festival, the Consualia, which included horse races. This link might stem from the vital role of water in nurturing the land, akin to how horses were essential in agriculture and transportation.

In art and literature, Neptune is frequently portrayed as a majestic figure, commanding the seas and waterways, reflecting his role as a powerful force of nature within the Roman pantheon. His temples and shrines were often located near bodies of water, emphasizing his close association with this vital element. As a god of such a fundamental aspect of the natural world, Neptune occupied an essential place in Roman mythology and religion, embodying the might and majesty of the waters that surrounded and sustained Roman civilization.

Minerva

In Roman mythology, Minerva is a revered goddess, embodying wisdom, strategic warfare, the arts, and crafts. She is one of the major deities in the Roman pantheon and is part of the Capitoline Triad along with Jupiter and Juno, reflecting her high status among the Roman gods. Minerva's role in Roman society is multifaceted, encompassing intellectual pursuits, strategic aspects of war, and various forms of artistic and practical skills.

Minerva is often portrayed as a figure of serenity and power, equipped with armor and a helmet, signifying her martial prowess, yet her primary association is not with the brutality of war but with the strategy and skills required in battle. Her domain extends beyond the battlefield, encapsulating the wisdom and knowledge necessary for statecraft and governance.

Moreover, Minerva is celebrated as the patroness of artisans, craftsmen, teachers, and scholars, highlighting her connection to the arts and education. Her influence is seen in various aspects of Roman culture, from literature and poetry to the practical skills of weaving and metallurgy. The festival of Quinquatria, held in her honor, was a time for artists, students, and tradespeople to seek her blessings and celebrate her contributions to their crafts.

Minerva's temples and altars were often centers of intellectual and artistic activity, underscoring her role as a nurturer of wisdom, creativity, and skill. As a goddess of such diverse yet interconnected realms, Minerva held a unique and revered place in Roman mythology, representing the harmonious balance between intellectual pursuits, practical skills, and the strategic aspects of life, both in peace and war.

Mars

In Roman mythology, Mars is a central and revered deity, known primarily as the god of war, but his influence extends far beyond the battlefield. Unlike war gods in many mythologies who are often associated solely with the chaos and destruction of war, Mars holds a more complex and multifaceted role in Roman culture. He is also a guardian of agriculture and a symbol of the vitality and survival of the community.

Mars' dual role as a god of war and agriculture reflects the early Roman society's dependence on both military prowess and agricultural success. In times of war, Mars was invoked for his martial strength, courage, and strategic skills. He was regarded as the quintessential embodiment of Roman military virtues, protecting the state and leading its armies to victory. In times of peace, however, his connection to agriculture became more pronounced. He was honored as a vital force that nurtured the land, ensuring the growth and abundance of crops, which was essential for the sustenance of the Roman people.

The month of March, named after Mars, encapsulates his dual nature. It was the traditional start of the military campaign season, as well as a crucial time for the commencement of agricultural work. The festivals held in his honor, such as the Feriae Marti in March and the Armilustrium in October, celebrate both aspects of his divine influence.

Mars was also seen as a father figure, often referred to as the father of Romulus and Remus, the legendary founders of Rome, which further solidified his position as a protector of the Roman state and its people. In Roman iconography, Mars is often depicted as a strong, armored warrior, but his symbols also include agricultural motifs, underscoring his connection to the land and its fertility. As a god of war and agriculture, Mars embodies the strength, resilience, and the dual priorities of early Roman society—military success and agricultural prosperity.

Venus

In Roman mythology, Venus is celebrated as the goddess of love, beauty, desire, and fertility. Her significance in the Roman pantheon extends beyond these domains, embodying the complexities of attraction, romance, and the generative forces of nature. Venus's role in Roman culture and religion is multifaceted, reflecting various aspects of human and natural life.

Venus was revered not only as a symbol of romantic and erotic love but also as a patroness of civic harmony and prosperity. She was invoked in various rituals and festivals, like the Veneralia, to promote beauty, love, and seduction, as well as to ensure the fertility of gardens and fields. Her influence on matters of the heart was profound, with Romans seeking her favor in their romantic pursuits and marriages.

Moreover, Venus held a significant place in Roman state religion. She was regarded as the divine ancestor of the Roman people through her son Aeneas, the legendary hero who escaped the fall of Troy and whose descendants were believed to have founded Rome. This lineage was especially emphasized by the Julian family, to which Julius Caesar belonged, claiming direct descent from Venus through Aeneas, lending a divine legitimacy to their rule.

In art and literature, Venus is often portrayed as a figure of captivating beauty and grace, reflecting her association with the aesthetic and alluring aspects of life. Yet, her depictions also suggest a deeper connection with the natural world, seen in her role as a symbol of fertility and the generative powers of nature.

As a goddess who transcended the boundaries between the personal and the political, between nature and human experience, Venus occupied a unique and revered place in Roman mythology. She was a deity who influenced not only the private aspects of love and beauty but also the broader spheres of social harmony and the continuity of the Roman lineage.

Apollo

In Roman mythology, Apollo stands as a multifaceted deity of significant importance, known for his association with the sun, healing, music, poetry, prophecy, and the arts. Unique among the Roman gods, Apollo retains his Greek name, indicating the deep cultural exchange between Rome and the Hellenic world. As a god of the sun, Apollo is envisioned as driving his chariot across the sky, bringing light and warmth to the earth, symbolizing clarity, truth, and reason.

Beyond his solar attributes, Apollo plays a crucial role as a god of healing and medicine. He is invoked for protection against diseases and for the healing of the sick, embodying the hope for health and well-being. His association with prophecy and oracles, particularly the Oracle at Delphi, further emphasizes his role as a deity of knowledge and foresight, guiding individuals and communities through his divine insights.

Apollo's influence extends to the realm of arts and culture. He is revered as the patron god of music, poetry, and the arts, symbolizing the beauty and harmony of creative expression. Festivals dedicated to Apollo, such as the Apollonian Games, celebrated these aspects, combining athletic competitions with artistic performances, highlighting his dual nature as a god of physical prowess and artistic mastery.

In Roman iconography, Apollo is often depicted as a youthful and handsome figure, embodying the ideals of beauty and perfection. He is frequently shown with a lyre, representing his patronage of music and the arts, and with a bow, symbolizing his ability to bring disease or health, as per his dual role as a bringer of plague and a healer.

Apollo's multifaceted nature reflects the Roman admiration for a harmonious balance between physical health, intellectual prowess, and artistic achievement. As such, he occupies a unique and significant place in Roman mythology, bridging the earthly and the divine, and influencing various aspects of Roman life and culture.

Diana

In Roman mythology, Diana is a revered goddess known for her association with the hunt, wilderness, and the moon. She is celebrated as a protector of the natural world and as a guardian of women, particularly during childbirth. Diana's role as a huntress embodies the Roman admiration for the skills of tracking, archery, and the understanding of the natural world, making her a symbol of independence and mastery over the wild.

As a moon goddess, Diana represents the luminous and enigmatic aspects of the night. She is often depicted with a crescent moon, emphasizing her connection to this celestial body and its cyclical nature. This aspect of Diana also symbolizes her role in overseeing the natural rhythms and cycles of life, aligning her with themes of femininity and fertility.

In her capacity as a guardian of women and children, Diana holds a special place in Roman culture. She is invoked for protection during childbirth, embodying the nurturing and protective qualities associated with motherhood. This aspect further cements her status as a deity closely tied to the vital processes of life and nature.

Diana's temples and sacred groves were often located in the heart of nature, reflecting her deep connection with the wilderness and its creatures. The most famous of these was the sanctuary at Lake Nemi, known as "Diana's Mirror," which served as a center for her worship and a place of asylum.

Despite her association with the wild and untamed aspects of the world, Diana was also integrated into the urban life of Rome. She was revered as a protector of the community, with her temples serving as places of refuge for slaves and the downtrodden, highlighting her role as a champion of the marginalized and vulnerable.

In Roman art, Diana is often portrayed as a huntress, carrying a bow and quiver, accompanied by a deer or hunting dogs. This portrayal not only emphasizes her mastery over the hunt but also her connection to the animal kingdom and the natural world. As a goddess of the hunt, the moon, and childbirth, Diana held a unique and revered place in Roman mythology, symbolizing the strength, independence, and nurturing power inherent in the natural world and the cycles of life.

Vulcan

In Roman mythology, Vulcan is the god of fire, including the fire of volcanoes, metalworking, and craftsmanship. His role in the pantheon is unique, as he is the divine smith and patron of artisans, particularly those involved in metalwork and the forge. Vulcan's association with fire and metallurgy symbolizes the transformative power of these elements, both in terms of physical materials and in broader metaphorical terms.

As a god of fire and craftsmanship, Vulcan is credited with creating weapons for the gods and heroes, forging masterpieces in his workshop that are both powerful and artistically exquisite. His skills are not limited to warfare; he is also revered for his ability to craft beautiful and intricate objects of art, demonstrating the Romans' appreciation for the combination of utility and beauty in craftsmanship.

Vulcan's temples and festivals, such as the Vulcanalia celebrated on August 23rd, reflect his importance in Roman society. The Vulcanalia was especially significant as it was a time to prevent destructive fires by offering sacrifices to Vulcan. Given the prevalence and danger of fires in ancient Rome, Vulcan's worship was not only a matter of religious devotion but also a practical necessity for the protection of the community.

In Roman iconography, Vulcan is often depicted with a blacksmith's hammer and anvil, highlighting his role as the master of fire and metalworking. Despite his immense skills and power, Vulcan is also portrayed as having a physical disability, which sets him apart from other gods and signifies his unique position within the Roman pantheon.

Vulcan's significance extends beyond his craftsmanship and control over fire. He represents the transformative power of fire and the importance of skilled labor and artistic ability in Roman culture. His worship underscores the value the Romans placed on mastery of craft and the protective aspects of fire, both in its potential for destruction and its essential role in forging and shaping materials.

Vesta

In Roman mythology, Vesta is a revered goddess embodying the hearth, home, and family. As one of the most significant deities in the Roman pantheon, her role extends beyond the physical hearth to symbolize the fire at the heart of community and family life. Vesta's presence in the household and the state is fundamental, representing the warmth, light, and stability that the hearth provides.

Vesta's importance is highlighted in her worship and the role of her priestesses, the Vestal Virgins. These priestesses were tasked with maintaining the sacred fire in the Temple of Vesta in Rome. This fire was not just a symbol of Vesta's presence but was also considered vital for the well-being and continuity of Rome. The eternal flame was a symbol of the eternal city itself, and its maintenance was a sacred duty that was believed to be linked to the fortune and prosperity of Rome.

The festival of Vestalia, held in her honor in June, was an important event in the Roman religious calendar. During this time, the inner sanctum of her temple was opened for women to offer sacrifices for the well-being of their families, emphasizing Vesta's role in domestic life and the protection of the home.

Unlike many other Roman deities, Vesta was not depicted in human form. Her presence was represented by the sacred flame, reflecting her role as an abstract embodiment of security and domestic harmony. As the goddess of the hearth, Vesta was central to daily life in Rome, with her flame serving as a constant reminder of the importance of the home and community in Roman society.

Vesta's worship reflects the deep significance of the hearth and home in Roman culture, symbolizing not only familial bonds and domestic stability but also the communal and enduring nature of Roman society. As such, she occupied a unique and revered place in Roman mythology, as the guardian of the hearth and the sustainer of domestic and civic harmony.

Mercury

In Roman mythology, Mercury is a multifaceted deity known as the messenger of the gods, as well as the god of commerce, travelers, and thieves. His role in the Roman pantheon is diverse, reflecting his adaptability, cunning, and dexterity. Mercury is characterized by his speed and mobility, often depicted with winged sandals and a winged helmet, which allow him to travel swiftly between the divine and mortal worlds.

As the messenger of the gods, Mercury is responsible for conveying divine messages to mortals, serving as a bridge between the celestial and earthly realms. His role as a communicator and intermediary makes him a crucial figure in Roman mythology, facilitating the interaction between gods and humans.

In his capacity as the god of commerce, Mercury oversees trade and the exchange of goods, symbolizing the flow of commerce and the prosperity it brings. Merchants and traders often sought his protection and blessings for successful business endeavors. This aspect of his deity reflects the importance of trade and commerce in Roman society and the value placed on economic prosperity.

Mercury's association with travelers stems from his role as a guide and protector for those journeying or undertaking new ventures. His protection was sought by those embarking on travels, especially in uncertain or risky circumstances. This role also extends to his patronage of thieves and tricksters, highlighting his cunning and strategic nature.

Festivals in honor of Mercury, such as the Mercuralia celebrated on May 15th, involved rituals like the sprinkling of water on the heads of merchants and their merchandise for luck and prosperity. This further underscores his role in the everyday lives of the Romans, connecting the divine with the practical and commercial aspects of society.

Mercury's dynamic nature, encompassing aspects of communication, commerce, and travel, reflects the complex and interconnected nature of Roman society and the pantheon. As a messenger and mediator, he bridges the gap between gods and mortals, while as a patron of commerce and travel, he represents the vital flow of goods, information, and people in the Roman world.

Ceres

In Roman mythology, Ceres is a highly revered goddess, embodying agriculture, grain crops, fertility, and motherly relationships. As the deity who presides over the growth and nourishment provided by agriculture, her role is central to Roman society, reflecting the fundamental importance of the harvest and the earth's bounty for the sustenance of life.

Ceres' association with agriculture extends beyond the mere growth of crops; she is deeply intertwined with the cycle of life and death, renewal, and sustenance. Her worship is integral to Roman agricultural rites and festivals, which are crucial for ensuring a bountiful harvest and, by extension, the well-being and prosperity of the Roman people. The most notable of these celebrations is the Cerealia, a festival held in April, dedicated to honoring Ceres and seeking her blessings for the growth of crops and the fertility of the land.

In addition to her agricultural aspects, Ceres is also revered as a goddess of motherly love and care, reflecting the nurturing aspect of the earth. Her role in this capacity extends to the protection and well-being of women, particularly in their roles as mothers and caretakers, further emphasizing her maternal qualities.

Ceres' importance in Roman mythology is also reflected in the Roman concept of 'Ceres' Law,' which pertains to the laws of marriage and the rights of parents over their children, highlighting her influence over personal and familial welfare.

As the patroness of agriculture, fertility, and motherhood, Ceres holds a position of great honor and significance in Roman religion. Her temples and shrines are places where people seek her favor for the fertility of the fields and the well-being of their families. In art and culture, Ceres is often depicted with symbols of the harvest, such as sheaves of wheat or a cornucopia, signifying abundance and nourishment. Through her various roles, Ceres embodies the nurturing power of the earth and the life-sustaining aspects of nature, crucial for the survival and prosperity of Roman society.

Two Other Primary Deities

While not considered Dii Consentes, these two deities are often mentioned in the same breath, as they were also widely recognized and worshipped by the Romans.

Bacchus

In Roman mythology, Bacchus is the god of wine, festivity, and ecstasy. His role is deeply intertwined with the vineyard, the mysteries of winemaking, and the uninhibited freedom that comes with intoxication. As a deity, Bacchus represents not only the physical process of viticulture and wine production but also the social and spiritual aspects associated with wine consumption.

Bacchus is often depicted as a youthful, vibrant figure, embodying the joy and abandon that can accompany wine drinking. He is the patron of revelry and the liberator of inhibitions, often associated with the wild, ecstatic celebrations known as Bacchanalia. These festivals, held in his honor, were characterized by music, dance, and a freedom from societal norms, reflecting the transformative power of wine and its ability to transcend the ordinary confines of life.

Beyond the aspects of festivity and intoxication, Bacchus also symbolizes the cycle of growth and decay inherent in nature, as seen in the lifecycle of the grapevine. He is thus a figure of both life and fertility, as well as a symbol of the powerful and sometimes unpredictable forces of nature.

In Roman society, Bacchus was revered not only for his association with wine and merriment but also for the communal bonding and spiritual ecstasy his worship facilitated. His cult provided an outlet for expression and release in the often rigid structures of Roman life. His festivals and rituals, while at times viewed with suspicion by Roman authorities for their ecstatic nature, played a significant role in the religious and cultural landscape of Rome.

Bacchus, as a god of wine, ecstasy, and the vitality of life, held a unique and significant place in Roman mythology, representing the dual nature of wine as both a symbol of civilization and culture, as well as a force for uninhibited joy and the breaking of conventional boundaries.

Pluto

In Roman mythology, Pluto is the god of the underworld and the afterlife, presiding over the realm of the dead. His domain is the dark and mysterious world beneath the earth, where souls go after leaving the mortal world. Pluto's role as the ruler of the underworld makes him a figure of awe and reverence, embodying the finality and inevitability of death, as well as the concept of resurrection and the cycle of life and death.

Despite his fearsome reputation, Pluto is also seen as a god of wealth, due to the riches of the earth (like precious metals and fertile soil) being under his domain. This aspect of his deity reflects the belief that from the underworld come the materials that can enrich the living world. This dual role aligns Pluto with both the darkest aspects of existence and the potential for growth and renewal that comes from beneath the earth.

The worship of Pluto in Roman religion was often intertwined with rituals and beliefs surrounding death, burial, and the afterlife. He was respected and sometimes feared, but also recognized as a necessary part of the natural order, overseeing the cycle of life and death that was central to Roman religious understanding.

In Roman art and literature, Pluto is often depicted as a regal and stern ruler, holding a bident or a cornucopia, symbolizing his power over the underworld and his association with earthly wealth. His character in mythology is complex, embodying the Roman respect for the power of death and the mysteries of the afterlife, while also representing the fertility and wealth that comes from the depths of the earth.

As the god of the underworld, Pluto plays a crucial role in Roman mythology, embodying the inevitability of death and the hope for life after death. His presence in Roman culture serves as a reminder of the cycle of life and death and the belief in the continuity of the soul beyond the mortal realm.

Minor Deities

Aurora

In Roman mythology, Aurora is the personification of the dawn, heralding the arrival of the sun each morning. As the goddess of dawn, she is responsible for bringing the first light of day, opening the gates of heaven for her brother Sol, the sun god, to ride his chariot across the sky. Aurora's role is crucial in the daily cycle of day and night, symbolizing renewal, hope, and the beginning of all things.

Aurora is often depicted as a radiant, beautiful figure, flying across the sky, announcing the arrival of daylight and dispersing the darkness of night. Her imagery is associated with renewal and rejuvenation, as each day is seen as a new beginning. In Roman art and literature, she is sometimes shown riding a chariot, illuminating the sky and the earth below with her gentle light.

Beyond her physical representation of the dawn, Aurora also embodies the Roman ideals of renewal and the endless cycles of time. Each of her appearances marks not just the start of a new day but also represents the perpetual rhythm of nature and the universe. In some Roman myths, Aurora is involved in several love stories, often with mortal men, symbolizing the fleeting nature of her early morning appearances.

Aurora's presence in Roman mythology reflects the significance the Romans placed on the natural order, the passage of time, and the transition from darkness to light. As the goddess of dawn, she holds a unique and enchanting position in the Roman pantheon, capturing the eternal beauty and hope that each new day brings.

Bellona

In Roman mythology, Bellona is a formidable goddess of war, often associated with martial vigor and the various aspects of warfare. Distinct in her own right, Bellona is considered a counterpart to Mars, the god of war, complementing his martial aspects with her own fierce and warlike nature. She embodies the aggressive and tumultuous aspects of battle, including the chaos and fury that accompany warfare.

Bellona's role in the Roman pantheon extends to being a patroness of soldiers and a symbol of the ferocity and bravery required in combat. Her temples were places where war councils were held and where Roman legions would gather before departing for military campaigns. The rituals associated with Bellona often involved war dances and the symbolic spilling of blood, reflecting her connection with the visceral nature of war.

In Roman iconography, Bellona is typically depicted as a warrior goddess, armed and ready for battle, often wearing a helmet and carrying a sword, spear, or shield. This portrayal emphasizes her martial prowess and her role as an instigator of warfare. She is seen as an embodiment of the warrior spirit, inspiring courage and strength in soldiers.

The worship of Bellona was particularly significant during times of conflict, as she was invoked for victory in battle and for the strength and resilience of the Roman military. Her presence in Roman mythology highlights the importance of warfare in Roman society and the reverence for the virtues of courage, strength, and military prowess. Bellona's fierce and warlike nature made her a revered deity in the Roman pantheon, symbolizing the aggressive and protective aspects of warfare.

Faunus

In Roman mythology, Faunus is a rustic god associated with the countryside, forests, and agriculture. Often regarded as a protector of farmers and shepherds, Faunus is seen as a benevolent deity who ensures the fertility of the land and the well-being of livestock. He is also connected to the wild and untamed aspects of nature, embodying the chaotic and unpredictable side of the natural world.

Faunus is often depicted as a humanoid figure with some animalistic features, such as horns and a tail, symbolizing his close association with nature and wildlife. His character is somewhat akin to that of a trickster, known for being playful, mischievous, and sometimes even frightening, especially in his interactions with humans.

The Romans celebrated Faunus through various festivals and rituals, the most notable being the Lupercalia, a fertility festival held in February. During this celebration, priests called Luperci would conduct purification and fertility rites to honor Faunus and promote the health and fertility of the people and the fields. The festival involved feasting, the sacrifice of goats, and playful, ritualistic whippings with strips of goatskin, which believed to promote fertility.

Faunus was also revered as a prophetic deity, believed to communicate divine messages through dreams and omens. His role as a communicator between the divine and the mortal realms further enhanced his significance in Roman religion.

As a god of the natural world, Faunus embodies the Romans' understanding of and respect for nature's dual aspects: its nurturing, life-giving side, and its wild, untamed essence. He represents the close bond between human society and the natural environment, emphasizing the need for balance and harmony with the natural world. His worship reflects the importance of agriculture in Roman life, as well as the reverence for the mysterious and uncontrolled aspects of nature.

Flora

In Roman mythology, Flora is the goddess of flowers, spring, and fertility. Her role is deeply intertwined with the blooming of plants and the renewal of life that comes with spring. As a deity, Flora is responsible for ensuring the growth of flowers and plants, symbolizing the cycle of life, renewal, and the beauty of nature.

Flora's festival, the Floralia, held annually in late April through early May, was a time of great festivity and celebration, reflecting the joy and abundance of spring. The festival included floral displays, theatrical performances, games, and licentious dances, symbolizing the reawakening of life and nature. It was also a time for the Romans to pay homage to Flora, seeking her blessings for bountiful harvests and the fertility of the land.

In Roman art and literature, Flora is often depicted as a youthful, beautiful goddess adorned with flowers and surrounded by a lush, blooming landscape. This imagery highlights her connection to the vitality and beauty of the natural world, particularly the flowering plants that herald the arrival of spring.

Flora's significance in Roman culture goes beyond her association with flowers and vegetation. She embodies the Romans' appreciation for the natural world's beauty and fertility. As a goddess of spring and renewal, Flora represents the promise of rebirth and the rejuvenating power of nature, a symbol of hope and the continuous cycle of life. Her worship reflects the importance of agriculture and fertility in Roman society, as well as the cultural value placed on the beauty and bounty of the natural world.

Fortuna

In Roman mythology, Fortuna is the goddess of fortune, luck, and fate, wielding considerable influence over the success and prosperity of individuals and the state. Her role is multifaceted, encompassing both the good fortune that brings prosperity and the unpredictable twists of fate that can lead to downfall. As such, Fortuna is revered and feared in equal measure, embodying the capricious nature of chance and the unpredictability of life's fortunes.

Fortuna's worship was widespread in Rome, with numerous temples and shrines dedicated to her. She was invoked by all strata of Roman society, from emperors and soldiers to merchants and farmers, each seeking her favor and benevolence in their endeavors. The Festival of Fortuna, celebrated in June, was a significant event, marked by games and offerings to appease and honor the goddess, in hopes of securing her favor.

In Roman art and iconography, Fortuna is often depicted holding a cornucopia, symbolizing abundance and prosperity, and a rudder, signifying her ability to steer the fate of individuals and the course of events. She is sometimes shown with a wheel, representing the ever-changing nature of fortune — sometimes on the rise, sometimes on the descent.

Fortuna's significance in Roman culture extends beyond mere superstition. She embodies the Roman understanding of the unpredictability of life and the role of chance in human affairs. Her worship reflects the Romans' desire to understand and influence the forces that shaped their lives, both in the personal sphere and in the broader context of the state. As the goddess of fortune, Fortuna represents the hopes and fears associated with the unforeseeable nature of fate, playing a crucial role in the Roman worldview and its approach to destiny and luck.

Luna

In Roman mythology, Luna is the personification of the Moon, playing a significant role as the goddess of this celestial body. She represents not just the physical moon that lights the night sky, but also the various phases of the lunar cycle and their influence on the earth, particularly on water bodies and agricultural cycles. Luna is often depicted as a beautiful goddess, driving a chariot across the sky, illuminating the darkness with her gentle light.

Luna's influence extends to various aspects of Roman life and culture. She is associated with the feminine, the rhythmic passage of time, and the subtle powers of the night. Her phases – new moon, waxing moon, full moon, and waning moon – are seen as powerful symbols of renewal, growth, fulfillment, and decline, mirroring the cycles of nature and human life.

In Roman art and literature, Luna is often depicted with a crescent moon, highlighting her connection to the lunar phases. She is sometimes shown riding a chariot pulled by horses or oxen, traversing the heavens and bringing the night. This imagery emphasizes her role as a celestial deity and her dominion over the night sky.

Luna's worship was not as prominent as that of some other Roman deities, but she held an important place in Roman mythology and religion. She was revered for her beauty and her soft, nurturing light, contrasting with the harsher light of her brother Sol, the sun god. In some Roman traditions, Luna was also associated with various forms of divination and prophecy, believed to hold insight into the mysteries and the unknown.

As the goddess of the Moon, Luna embodies the Roman fascination with the celestial bodies and their influence on the natural world and human affairs. She represents the beauty and mystery of the night sky, and her presence in Roman mythology highlights the importance of the moon in Roman culture, both as a physical entity and a symbol of the cycles of time and change.

Pomona

In Roman mythology, Pomona is the goddess specifically associated with fruit trees, gardens, and orchards. Her role is distinct and important in the Roman pantheon, as she oversees the cultivation and harvest of fruit, symbolizing the abundance and fertility of the earth. Unlike many other Roman deities, Pomona's focus is not broad but deeply specialized, emphasizing the Romans' appreciation and reverence for the cultivation of fruits and the care of orchards.

Pomona is often depicted as a nurturing figure, surrounded by fruits and holding gardening tools, such as a pruning knife, symbolizing her mastery and care in the art of fruit cultivation. Her imagery represents the nurturing aspect of nature and the bountiful gifts that careful and respectful cultivation can bring.

Her worship was particularly significant to Roman gardeners and fruit farmers, who looked to her for guidance in their work and for ensuring the health and abundance of their crops. Pomona's festivals were likely low-key and agricultural in nature, focusing on the practical aspects of her domain.

The myth of Pomona also includes her relationship with Vertumnus, the god of seasons, change, and plant growth. Vertumnus, in his love for Pomona, is said to have disguised himself to gain access to her orchard. Their story emphasizes the importance of careful cultivation and the change of seasons in the growth of fruits, reflecting the interconnectedness of natural cycles and agricultural practices.

As a deity, Pomona represents the Romans' agricultural skills and their close relationship with the land, particularly in the cultivation of fruit. Her specialized role underscores the value placed on agriculture in Roman society and the understanding of its critical role in providing sustenance and prosperity. Pomona's presence in Roman mythology highlights the importance of harmony with nature and the respect for the careful tending of the earth's resources.

Portunus

In Roman mythology, Portunus (or Portumnus) is the god of keys, doors, and livestock, particularly associated with ports and harbors. His role as a protector of gates and harbors highlights the Romans' deep connection with trade and seafaring, reflecting the importance of these activities in the growth and prosperity of Rome. Portunus' domain over doors and gates also extends to a more symbolic level, encompassing the idea of transitions and the opening and closing of opportunities, both literally and metaphorically.

Portunus is often depicted with keys, an attribute that symbolizes his role as a guardian and opener of doors, both in a physical and spiritual sense. His connection with harbors makes him an important deity for sailors and merchants, who sought his protection for their ships and cargo, ensuring safe passage and prosperous trade.

The worship of Portunus in Rome included the celebration of the Portunalia, a festival held on August 17th. During this festival, keys were thrown into a fire as a sacrifice to Portunus, seeking his blessings for the protection and prosperity of their homes and stores. The festival was an important event, especially for those whose livelihoods were connected to trade and travel.

Portunus' significance in Roman mythology is tied to the practical aspects of Roman life. His association with ports underscores the importance of trade and commerce in Roman society, while his guardianship of doors and gates reflects the Roman understanding of transitions, both in everyday life and in the broader journey of life itself. As a deity, Portunus embodies the Romans' appreciation for the safekeeping and protection of their homes, possessions, and their comings and goings, playing a crucial role in the everyday life of the Roman people.

Quirinus

In Roman mythology, Quirinus is a deity whose origins and role evolved significantly over time. Originally, Quirinus was a Sabine god of war and later became associated with the Roman state and its community. As Rome expanded and assimilated the Sabine people, Quirinus was absorbed into the Roman pantheon and eventually identified with the deified form of Romulus, the legendary founder of Rome.

Quirinus' role in Roman religion is closely tied to the civic and communal aspects of Roman society. He is one of the three major deities of the Archaic Triad, along with Jupiter and Mars, worshipped at the Capitoline Temple, which reflects his significance in early Roman religion. As a god of the Roman state, Quirinus symbolizes the strength and integrity of the Roman community, particularly in its aspects of citizenship, social organization, and collective Roman identity.

The cult of Quirinus emphasized the well-being and stability of the Roman state. His temple on the Quirinal Hill, one of the seven hills of Rome, was a significant place of worship. The

Quirinalia festival, celebrated on February 17th, was dedicated to him and was a time for Romans to reaffirm their communal bonds and pray for the health and prosperity of the community.

In Roman iconography, Quirinus is often depicted as a bearded figure wearing a toga and carrying religious and civic symbols, emphasizing his role as a protector of the state and the civic unity of the Roman people. His association with the legendary Romulus further enshrines him in the mythic and historical narrative of Rome, symbolizing the city's founding, growth, and the virtues of its people.

As a deity, Quirinus represents the Romans' respect for their cultural and civic origins, their sense of community, and the social cohesion necessary for the state's survival and prosperity. His evolution from a Sabine god of war to a Roman deity of the state reflects the fluid nature of Roman religious practices and the incorporation of foreign deities into the Roman pantheon as Rome expanded its influence.

Sol

In Roman mythology, Sol is the personification of the Sun, a powerful and vital deity who governs the light and warmth essential to life on Earth. As the god of the sun, Sol's role is central to the Roman understanding of the cosmos and the natural world. He is seen as the one who drives the sun across the sky in his chariot, bringing daylight to the world and governing the passage of time marked by days, seasons, and years.

Sol's influence extends beyond the mere physical aspects of the sun. He is associated with vision, enlightenment, and knowledge, symbolizing the illumination of the mind and the revelation of truth. This connection between the physical light of the sun and the metaphorical light of knowledge and truth is a significant aspect of Sol's role in Roman culture.

The worship of Sol was important in Roman religion, and his cult grew particularly prominent during the later periods of the Roman Empire. The Emperor Aurelian established a formal cult of Sol Invictus ("Unconquered Sun") in the 3rd century CE, which became one of the major deities of the Roman state. The festival of Sol Invictus, celebrated on December 25th, was an important event, marking the rebirth of the sun after the winter solstice and symbolizing the renewal of light and life.

In Roman art, Sol is often depicted riding a quadriga, a four-horse chariot, across the sky. He is typically shown with a radiant halo or crown, embodying the glory and power of the sun. As a solar deity, Sol holds a significant place in Roman mythology, representing the life-giving energy of the sun, the passage of time, and the intellectual and spiritual illumination it brings. His worship reflects the Romans' reverence for the sun as a vital force in the natural world and a symbol of divine power and insight.

Somnus

In Roman mythology, Somnus is the personification of sleep, embodying the concept and state of slumber. As a deity, Somnus holds sway over the realm of dreams and unconsciousness, governing the nightly repose of both gods and mortals. His role is integral to the natural cycle of day and night, rest and wakefulness, reflecting the Roman understanding of the necessity of rest for rejuvenation and health.

Somnus is often depicted as a gentle, quiet figure, emphasizing the peaceful nature of sleep. He is sometimes shown with poppies and other hypnotic plants, symbolizing the sedative qualities associated with inducing sleep. In art, Somnus is occasionally represented as a youthful, serene figure, often with wings, suggesting the fleeting and elusive nature of sleep.

The Roman myths surrounding Somnus highlight his ability to control and influence the realm of dreams. He is capable of sending visions and messages through dreams, weaving fantasies and illusions in the minds of sleepers. Despite his seemingly passive nature, Somnus wields significant power, as sleep is essential for the restoration of body and mind, impacting the well-being and functioning of all beings.

Somnus' presence in Roman mythology underscores the importance the Romans placed on the balance between activity and rest. Sleep, under the dominion of Somnus, is not merely a state of inactivity but a vital necessity, providing rest, renewal, and access to the mysterious and insightful world of dreams. As the god of sleep, Somnus represents the essential, restorative aspects of slumber, highlighting its significance in the cycle of daily life and its influence on the human psyche.

Terminus

In Roman mythology, Terminus is the god of boundary markers, symbolizing the demarcation of property and the respect for boundaries, both physical and metaphorical. As a deity, Terminus is unique in that he represents a specific, tangible aspect of Roman life: the marking and protection of boundaries, whether they be for private lands, sacred spaces, or even the boundaries of the city of Rome itself.

Terminus was often represented not in human form but as a stone or a pillar, signifying the physical markers used by the Romans to demarcate land. This representation underscores the sanctity and permanence of boundaries in Roman culture. The annual celebration of the Terminalia, held on February 23rd, was dedicated to honoring Terminus. During this festival, neighbors would gather to reaffirm their mutual respect for shared boundaries, often adorning boundary stones with garlands and making offerings to ensure the continued peace and respect between them.

The worship of Terminus also reflects the Roman legal and social emphasis on property rights and the importance of clearly defined and respected boundaries. His role in Roman religion is closely tied to the maintenance of order and peace within the community, ensuring that each person's property is respected and protected.

The significance of Terminus in Roman society extends to the idea of personal and civic limits. He embodies the concept of respecting one's limits and the importance of understanding and maintaining one's place within the social, political, and physical landscapes of Roman life. As the god of boundaries, Terminus represents the legal and social structures that define and protect individual and communal spaces, playing a crucial role in the orderly function of Roman society.

Trivia

In Roman mythology, Trivia is the goddess of crossroads, magic, and the night. Her name, derived from the Latin "trivium" (meaning "three roads"), signifies her association with the places where three roads meet, which were considered mystical and significant in ancient Rome. As the guardian of these crossroads, Trivia is believed to have special powers and insight, overseeing the literal and metaphorical paths one might take in life.

Trivia is often depicted as a mysterious and enigmatic figure, embodying the secretive and hidden aspects of the world. Her connection to the night and darkness ties her to the realm of the unknown and the supernatural. As a goddess of magic, she is invoked in matters of witchcraft and enchantments, holding sway over the more arcane and mystical aspects of existence.

The worship of Trivia includes practices and rituals that are shrouded in secrecy and often conducted at night or at crossroads, emphasizing her connection to the mystical and the hidden. She is considered a protector of witches and a guide for those who venture into the realms of magic and the unknown.

Trivia's role in Roman mythology goes beyond her association with magic and crossroads. She represents the idea of choice and the importance of decisions, especially at life's metaphorical crossroads. Her presence at the intersection of three roads symbolizes the multiple directions one's life can take and the inherent uncertainty and potential that such choices embody.

As a deity of crossroads, magic, and the night, Trivia occupies a unique and intriguing place in Roman mythology. She embodies the mystery and potential of the paths we choose in life, the hidden aspects of the world around us, and the mystical forces that lie just beyond the realm of the known. Her presence in Roman religion highlights the Romans' fascination with and respect for the mystical and the mysterious aspects of the world.

Vulturnus

In Roman mythology, Vulturnus is a lesser-known deity associated with the east wind. His role is primarily connected with the specific aspect of meteorology, representing one of the several wind gods, each governing a different direction of wind. As the god of the east wind, Vulturnus' influence is tied to the climatic and agricultural aspects of Roman life.

The east wind, under the dominion of Vulturnus, was often considered less favorable compared to other winds, sometimes associated with dry, hot weather that could be detrimental to crops and uncomfortable for people. This characterization reflects the Romans' keen observation of natural phenomena and their impact on agriculture and daily life.

While not among the most prominent deities in the Roman pantheon, Vulturnus' role in the control and representation of the east wind showcases the Roman tendency to personify and deify natural forces. His existence in Roman mythology underscores the importance the Romans placed on understanding and appeasing the various elements of the natural world, which were seen as vital to their well-being and prosperity.

In terms of worship and representation, Vulturnus, like other wind gods, did not receive the same level of attention as major deities like Jupiter or Mars. However, his presence in the pantheon signifies the Romans' desire to acknowledge and respect the diverse forces of nature that influenced their lives, from the grandeur of the sea and sky to the subtler, yet equally significant, directions of the wind. Vulturnus, as the personification of the east wind, embodies this intricate relationship between the Romans and the natural world.

Sylvanus

In Roman mythology, Sylvanus is a deity associated with woods, fields, and uncultivated land. He is revered as a protector of agriculture and a guardian of the boundaries between the wild, untamed parts of nature and the cultivated lands of the Roman people. Sylvanus embodies the spirit of the rural landscape, the forests, and the pastoral fields, playing an essential role in the lives of those who lived and worked in these areas.

As a god of the woodlands, Sylvanus is often depicted in Roman art and literature as a rustic figure, carrying a cypress branch or a pine wreath, symbols of the forest. He is sometimes shown accompanied by animals, emphasizing his connection to wildlife and nature. Sylvanus was not just a deity of the wilderness; he was also revered for his ability to protect crops, livestock, and the borders of fields and farms. His worship reflects the Roman understanding of the delicate balance between nature and agriculture, and the need to maintain harmony between these realms.

The cult of Sylvanus was particularly significant to Roman farmers, shepherds, and those living in rural areas. Small shrines and altars dedicated to him were common in the countryside, where people would offer prayers and sacrifices for his protection and favor. These practices underscored the importance of Sylvanus in ensuring the fertility of the land, the health of the forests, and the safety of those who dwelt within or near these domains.

Household Deities

Lares

In Roman mythology, the Lares are a group of deities representing household and family spirits. Each Roman household worshiped its own Lares, who were believed to protect the home and ensure the family's prosperity and well-being. These protective deities were deeply ingrained in the daily lives and domestic rituals of the Romans, embodying the sacredness of the family and the home.

The Lares were typically honored in small shrines within the home, known as Larariums. These shrines were often located in the atrium or the hearth, and daily offerings and prayers were made to appease and venerate the Lares. The offerings included food, wine, and incense, symbolizing the integration of the Lares into every aspect of household life.

Beyond the household, the concept of Lares extended to the larger community as well. There were Lares of crossroads (Lares Compitales), who were worshiped at intersections and communal spaces, and Lares of the city (Lares Praestites), who protected the entire community and were honored in public ceremonies.

The depiction of the Lares usually showed them as youthful, benevolent spirits, often seen holding a cornucopia or a patera (a shallow dish used for libations), symbolizing their role in bringing prosperity and blessings to the household. They were sometimes accompanied by a dog, representing loyalty and protection.

The worship of the Lares reflects the Roman emphasis on the importance of the family unit and the sanctity of the home. These deities were not high gods of grand mythology but intimate, familial spirits that safeguarded and nurtured the individual households and the broader community. The Lares played a crucial role in Roman religion, emphasizing the connection between the divine and the mundane aspects of daily life, and ensuring the continuity of family and community welfare through generations.

Penates

In Roman mythology, the Penates are deities associated with the household, specifically linked to the pantry and the storeroom, and are considered protectors of the family's provisions and wellbeing. Along with the Lares, they form an integral part of the domestic cult, deeply embedded in the daily life and religious practices of Roman families.

The Penates were believed to reside in the innermost part of the Roman home, where they were worshiped in the household shrine alongside the Lares. This shrine, known as the Lararium, was often placed in a prominent location, such as the kitchen or the hearth, signifying the central role of the Penates in the household's sustenance and prosperity. Offerings of food and wine were regularly made to them, reflecting their role in overseeing the family's nourishment and the abundance of the household.

In terms of their depiction, the Penates were often represented as a pair of young men, sometimes shown holding abundance symbols like cornucopias, plates of food, or drinking vessels. These representations underscore their association with the sustenance and the prosperity of the household.

Beyond their domestic role, the Penates also had a broader significance in Roman religion. They were sometimes considered protectors of the entire state, especially in early Roman history, and were honored in public ceremonies. Their worship underscores the importance of the family and the home in Roman culture, emphasizing the belief that the wellbeing of the state begins with the wellbeing of its individual households.

The Penates, as deities of the household pantry and storeroom, represent the Romans' deep connection to and reverence for the home as a sacred space. They embody the essential aspects of domestic life, ensuring the family's nourishment and the continuity of its prosperity and wellbeing. Their presence in Roman mythology highlights the importance placed on the family unit and the sanctity of the domestic sphere in Roman society.

Manes

In Roman mythology, the Manes are the spirits of the deceased, revered as protective ancestors. They played a significant role in Roman religion and were an integral part of the family's spiritual life. The concept of the Manes reflects the Romans' beliefs about death, the afterlife, and the enduring connection between the living and the dead.

The Manes were believed to reside in the underworld but were also thought to be present in the world of the living, particularly within the household. They were honored in domestic rituals and were thought to watch over and protect their living descendants. The presence of the Manes in the home was both a comforting and solemn reminder of familial lineage and the continuity of the family across generations.

One of the most important observances for the Manes was the Parentalia, an annual festival lasting from February 13th to February 21st, during which families honored their deceased ancestors. This festival involved visiting graves, offering sacrifices, and performing rites to appease and communicate with the spirits of the departed. The festival's conclusion, the Feralia on February 21st, was a public holiday dedicated to the collective honoring of the dead.

The Manes were often collectively invoked in prayers and were commonly referred to as "Di Manes," meaning "the divine dead." This designation highlights their revered status and the Romans' respect for the ancestral spirits. In contrast to some depictions of the underworld's spirits, the Manes were generally viewed as benevolent and protective, provided they were properly venerated and remembered.

The cult of the Manes underscores the importance of family, memory, and tradition in Roman culture. It reflects the belief in the continued presence and influence of ancestors in the lives of the living, emphasizing the moral and familial obligations of the living to remember and honor the dead. The Manes, as ancestral spirits, embody the Roman reverence for lineage, tradition, and the enduring bonds of family across the threshold of life and death.

CHAPTER 2:
OTHER CHARACTERS

In addition to the many deities mentioned in the previous chapter, Roman mythology is host to a wide array of other characters. These include demi-gods, monsters, nymphs, animals, mortals, and more! In this chapter we will introduce you to some of these characters that you will encounter in the later myths.

Aeneas

In Roman mythology, Aeneas is a legendary hero and a central figure in Rome's foundational myths. He is best known as the protagonist of Virgil's epic poem, the "Aeneid," which chronicles his journey from the war-torn city of Troy to the founding of what would eventually become the city of Rome. Aeneas is often depicted as a paragon of piety and duty, embodying the Roman virtues of devotion to family, gods, and country.

Aeneas' story begins with the fall of his native city, after which he embarks on a long and arduous journey, carrying his father Anchises and leading other refugees in search of a new homeland. His travels take him to various places around the Mediterranean, including Carthage, where he has a tragic love affair with Queen Dido. Guided by the will of the gods and his sense of duty, Aeneas eventually leaves Carthage to fulfill his destiny.

Upon arriving in Italy, Aeneas engages in battles and negotiations with local tribes, laying the groundwork for the establishment of Rome. He marries Lavinia, a local princess, which further cements his role in the foundation of the Roman people. His descendants, through his son Ascanius (also known as Iulus), are said to include Romulus and Remus, the legendary founders of Rome.

Aeneas' significance in Roman mythology and culture cannot be overstated. He is seen not just as a heroic figure of the past, but as a symbol of Roman ideals and identity. His journey, marked by trials, sacrifices, and a strong sense of destiny, reflects the Roman values of perseverance, loyalty, and commitment to a greater cause. Aeneas' story, as portrayed in the "Aeneid," serves as a national epic, linking Rome's origins to the ancient and venerable tradition of his journey, and establishing a sense of continuity, destiny, and divine favor for the Roman people.

Hercules

In Roman mythology, Hercules is celebrated as a hero of extraordinary strength and courage, renowned for his incredible feats and adventures. Adopted into Roman culture, Hercules became a symbol of strength, bravery, and heroism, deeply ingrained in Roman society and mythology. His most famous exploits are the Twelve Labors, a series of seemingly impossible tasks that he successfully completed, each showcasing his physical prowess, endurance, and cleverness.

Hercules' role in Roman mythology extends beyond his physical strength. He is also seen as a protector of mankind, using his formidable abilities to battle monstrous creatures and overcome great challenges. His feats often involved dealing with dangerous beasts like the Nemean Lion and the Lernaean Hydra, tasks that not only displayed his strength but also his determination and resourcefulness.

The Romans venerated Hercules not only as a hero but also as a god-like figure, and he was worshipped in various temples and sanctuaries across Rome and its territories. The cult of Hercules was one of the most popular and widespread in Roman religion, with the Hercules Magusanus being particularly revered among Roman soldiers.

In Roman art and literature, Hercules is often depicted with the skin of the Nemean Lion and carrying a club, his iconic attributes. His portrayal emphasized his heroic qualities and the virtues that the Romans most admired: bravery, perseverance in the face of adversity, and the ability to protect and serve the greater good.

Hercules' presence in Roman mythology highlights the Romans' admiration for heroes who embody physical strength and moral fortitude. His stories served not only as entertainment but also as moral examples, teaching the values of courage, hard work, and the importance of using one's abilities for the benefit of others. Hercules, in Roman culture, thus represents the ideal of heroism, deeply rooted in physical prowess and ethical conduct.

Romulus

In Roman mythology, Romulus is revered as the legendary founder and first king of Rome. His story is central to Rome's foundation myth, encapsulating the city's origins and the Roman virtues of strength, courage, and leadership. According to the myth, Romulus and his twin brother Remus were the sons of Rhea Silvia, a vestal virgin, and were believed to be descended from the gods. As infants, they were abandoned and left to die but were miraculously saved and suckled by a she-wolf. This iconic image of the twins being nurtured by a wolf has become a powerful symbol of Rome.

Romulus and Remus grew up to become natural leaders, eventually deciding to establish a city. However, a dispute arose over where to build the new city and who would rule it. This disagreement led to a tragic confrontation in which Romulus killed Remus, a narrative underscoring the themes of rivalry and the high stakes of leadership and power. Following this event, Romulus went on to found Rome, laying the first stones of what would become one of the greatest cities in history on the Palatine Hill.

As the first king of Rome, Romulus is credited with establishing many of its fundamental institutions, including the Roman Senate and the city's first legions and tribes. His rule is marked by a series of military conquests and expansion, as well as the establishment of social and political foundations that would shape Roman society for centuries.

Romulus' eventual disappearance and deification add a divine aspect to his legacy. He was said to have been taken up by the gods and worshipped as the deity Quirinus, further linking the city's political and spiritual beginnings to his extraordinary life and reign.

In Roman culture, Romulus is more than a mythological figure; he is a symbol of the city's strength, resilience, and destiny. His story, blending history with legend, embodies the Roman ideals of bravery, innovation, and the ability to overcome great odds. Romulus, as the founder of Rome, holds a place of honor in Roman history and mythology, representing the city's origins and its enduring spirit.

Remus

In Roman mythology, Remus holds a significant but tragic role as one of the co-founders of Rome and the twin brother of Romulus. The story of Remus begins with his and Romulus's miraculous survival as infants. According to legend, they were the sons of Rhea Silvia, a vestal virgin, and were abandoned and left to die. In a tale that has become emblematic of Rome's founding, they were saved and suckled by a she-wolf in the wilderness. This iconic image of the twins with the wolf is deeply ingrained in Roman symbolism and cultural identity.

Raised by a shepherd, Remus and Romulus grew up away from civilization, embodying the virtues of strength, courage, and natural leadership. As young men, they decided to establish a city, but disagreements arose over its location and leadership. This dispute culminated in a dramatic and fateful moment in Roman mythology: during an argument, Romulus killed Remus. This act of fratricide is a pivotal moment in the founding myth of Rome, underscoring themes of ambition, conflict, and the high price of establishing a new order.

Remus's death is a foundational tragedy in Roman history, marking the birth of Rome with a mix of triumph and sorrow. While Romulus went on to establish and rule the city, Remus's story serves as a reminder of the complexities and challenges involved in the creation of the Roman state. His character and fate illustrate the tensions between kinship and ambition, community and power, that would continue to play out throughout Rome's history.

In Roman culture, Remus, though overshadowed by his brother Romulus in terms of legacy, is still remembered as a key figure in Rome's mythical origins. His story represents not only the city's founding but also the inherent struggles and sacrifices involved in the birth and growth of a great civilization. Remus, as a central figure in the legendary narrative, contributes significantly to the mythos and identity of ancient Rome.

Camilla

In Roman mythology, Camilla is a celebrated female warrior known for her exceptional skill in combat and speed. She is most famously depicted in Virgil's epic, "The Aeneid," where she is a prominent figure in the latter part of the story. Camilla is the daughter of King Metabus and a princess of the Volsci, a tribe known for their martial prowess.

Camilla's backstory is marked by drama and resilience. Her father, Metabus, in a bid to save her from enemies, dedicated her to the service of the goddess Diana and raised her in the wilderness. Growing up in such an environment, Camilla became a formidable huntress and warrior, skilled in archery and able to move through the forest with incredible agility and speed. Her upbringing imbued her with the qualities of fierceness, independence, and a deep connection to the natural world.

In "The Aeneid," Camilla is a key ally of Turnus, the leader of the Rutuli, in his war against Aeneas and the Trojans. She leads a troop of cavalry into battle and is portrayed as a fierce and noble warrior, fearlessly charging into combat. Her prowess in battle is unmatched, and she plays a significant role in the conflict, striking fear in the hearts of her adversaries.

Camilla's character is notable not only for her martial skills but also for her dedication and loyalty to her cause and people. Her story, while ultimately tragic as she falls in battle, highlights the themes of heroism, sacrifice, and the valor of women in warfare.

Turnus

In Roman mythology, Turnus is a prominent figure known primarily through Virgil's epic, "The Aeneid." He is the king of the Rutulians, a tribe in Italy, and plays the role of a primary antagonist in the latter part of the poem. Turnus is characterized as a brave and powerful warrior, but his story is also marked by pride, passion, and a tragic end.

The conflict in "The Aeneid" that involves Turnus arises from the arrival of Aeneas and his Trojan followers in Italy, where they seek to establish a new homeland. Turnus opposes their settlement, partly motivated by his desire to marry Lavinia, the daughter of King Latinus. Lavinia is promised to Aeneas by her father, and this promise, influenced by divine will, sets the stage for the conflict between Aeneas and Turnus.

Turnus is a formidable opponent in battle, respected and feared for his prowess in combat. He is fiercely loyal to his people and passionate in defending his claim to Lavinia and his land against the Trojans. His courage and strength make him a worthy rival to Aeneas, and their conflict is one of the central themes of the epic.

Despite his bravery, Turnus' story is ultimately a tragic one. His refusal to yield to the will of the gods and his insistence on pursuing the war against Aeneas lead to his downfall. In the climactic battle of the epic, Turnus faces Aeneas in single combat, a duel that results in Turnus' death. His demise signifies the tragic consequences of pride and resistance to fate, themes that are central to "The Aeneid."

Numa Pompilius

Numa Pompilius holds a revered place in Roman mythology as the second king of Rome, succeeding Romulus. Unlike his predecessor, Numa is not celebrated for his martial achievements but rather for his wisdom, piety, and peaceful reign. According to Roman tradition, Numa was chosen as king due to his deep understanding of religious and philosophical matters, and his reign is characterized by the establishment of many of Rome's religious and legal institutions.

Born to the Sabines, an ancient people living near Rome, Numa was known for his just and religious nature. His reign marked a significant shift from the warlike period under Romulus to a time of peace and religious reform. Numa is credited with establishing numerous religious practices and priestly offices, including the Vestal Virgins and the Pontifex Maximus, the high priest of Rome. He is also associated with the introduction of important Roman religious rites and the construction of temples dedicated to various deities.

Numa's legislative contributions were equally significant. He is said to have instituted laws that sought to civilize public and private behavior, encouraging the Roman people to live righteous and pious lives. These laws were not just legal statutes but were imbued with religious significance, reinforcing the deeply intertwined nature of religion and law in Roman culture.

One of the key aspects of Numa's reign was his purported communication with the divine, particularly through the nymph Egeria. These interactions underscored his role as a divinely guided ruler, whose policies and reforms were seen as sanctioned by the gods.

In Roman mythology and history, Numa Pompilius is remembered as a wise ruler, a model of virtue and piety. His reign represents an idealized era of peace and religious devotion, setting a standard for future leaders and significantly shaping the religious and cultural fabric of Rome. His legacy in Roman culture is that of a philosopher-king who contributed profoundly to the moral and spiritual foundations of Roman society.

The Cumaean Sibyl

In Roman mythology, the Cumaean Sibyl holds a prominent role as a prophetess and priestess presiding over the Apollonian oracle at Cumae, near Naples. She is renowned for her oracular powers, granting prophecies and visions influenced by the god Apollo. Her reputation as a seer made her one of the most respected and feared figures in Roman religious life.

The Cumaean Sibyl is best known for her role in Virgil's "Aeneid," where she acts as a guide for the hero Aeneas during his journey to the Underworld. In this epic narrative, her deep knowledge of the divine and the mystical realms allows her to lead Aeneas safely through the challenges of the underworld, providing him with insight and prophecy about his future and the future of Rome.

Beyond her appearance in the "Aeneid," the Cumaean Sibyl is also famous for the Sibylline Books, a collection of prophetic writings said to have been offered to one of the early Roman kings. These books contained prophecies and guidance that were consulted by the Roman state in times of crisis. The Sibylline Books were kept in the temple of Jupiter on the Capitoline Hill and were guarded and interpreted by a special group of priests.

The Cumaean Sibyl's enduring legacy in Roman culture lies in her representation of divine wisdom and the mysterious nature of prophecy. She embodies the Roman belief in the power of divine revelation and its influence on human destiny. Her figure is shrouded in mystery and awe, reflecting the Romans' reverence for and fear of the unknown powers that shape their world and destiny.

Charon

In Roman mythology, Charon is the somber figure known as the ferryman of the dead. He plays a crucial role in the journey of souls to the afterlife. According to Roman beliefs about the afterlife, Charon is responsible for transporting the souls of the deceased across the rivers that separate the world of the living from the realm of the dead, such as the River Styx.

Charon is often depicted as an elderly man, grizzled and stern, conveying the solemn nature of his duty. He mans a ferry or a boat, and it is his task to guide the souls across the waters to their final resting place in the underworld. However, Charon only ferries those who can pay his fare, traditionally an obolus or a small coin. This payment is placed in the mouth of the deceased at burial, a practice reflecting the belief in the necessary preparation for the afterlife journey.

Cacus

In Roman mythology, Cacus is a fearsome creature, often portrayed as a fire-breathing giant or a monstrous humanoid. His story is best known from the tales of early Rome, particularly in connection with the legendary hero Hercules. Cacus represents the archetypal villain or monster in Roman folklore, embodying chaos, lawlessness, and the antithesis of Roman virtues.

Cacus lived in a cave in the Aventine Hill, in the region that would later become the city of Rome. He was infamous for terrorizing the countryside, stealing cattle, and spreading fear among the people. According to the legend, Cacus stole part of the cattle Hercules was herding – animals that Hercules had obtained during his tenth labor. To hide his theft, Cacus dragged the cattle backward into his cave, so their tracks would not lead back to him.

Hercules, however, discovered the theft and pursued Cacus to his lair. A fierce battle ensued between the hero and the monster, which culminated in Hercules slaying Cacus. This act of bravery by Hercules was celebrated by the local people and marked Hercules as a protector and hero.

The Harpies

In Roman mythology, the Harpies are fearsome creatures known for their role as agents of punishment and retribution. They are typically depicted as having the body of a bird and the face of a woman, embodying a terrifying blend of avian and human features. The Harpies are notorious for their swift, merciless actions, often swooping down from the sky to snatch or defile food, and are associated with the concept of justice, particularly in its more vengeful and unforgiving aspects.

The most famous account of the Harpies in Roman mythology appears in the story of the blind prophet Phineus, who was punished by the gods for revealing too much of the future to mortals. The Harpies were sent to torment him by stealing or defiling his food, leaving him in a state of constant hunger and misery. This story illustrates their role as instruments of divine punishment, enforcing the will of the gods and ensuring that mortal transgressions did not go unpunished.

Egeria

In Roman mythology, Egeria is a revered nymph known primarily for her role as a divine consort and advisor to Numa Pompilius, the second king of Rome. As a nymph, Egeria is associated with water sources and nature, embodying the sacred and prophetic aspects of natural springs and groves. Her story intertwines with the foundational narratives of Rome, especially in relation to its early religious and legal institutions.

Egeria provided Numa with knowledge and guidance, which he used to establish important religious rites, laws, and social customs in Rome. According to legend, Numa would meet Egeria in a sacred grove, where she imparted wisdom and divine insights. These encounters enabled Numa to introduce vital religious practices and to lay down laws that would shape the moral and spiritual fabric of Roman society. Egeria's influence was crucial in establishing the peaceful and religious aspects of Numa's reign, contrasting with the warlike period under his predecessor, Romulus.

Rhea Silvia

In Roman mythology, Rhea Silvia is a central figure in the foundation myth of Rome. She is most famously known as the mother of Romulus and Remus, the legendary twins associated with the founding of Rome. Rhea Silvia's story is one of tragedy, divine intervention, and the establishment of a great city.

Rhea Silvia was a vestal virgin and a daughter of Numitor, the former king of Alba Longa. Numitor was deposed by his brother Amulius, who then forced Rhea Silvia to become a vestal virgin, a role that required her to remain chaste. However, in the myth, Mars, the god of war, impregnated her, and she gave birth to the twins Romulus and Remus. Because of her broken vow of chastity – albeit enforced by divine will – and the threat they posed to Amulius's rule, the twins were ordered to be killed.

In a tale that has become central to Roman lore, the infants were set adrift on the river Tiber but were miraculously saved. They were discovered by a she-wolf who suckled them, and later a shepherd and his wife raised them. When the twins grew up, they overthrew Amulius, reinstated Numitor, and went on to found the city of Rome.

Rhea Silvia's role in Roman mythology is pivotal. She bridges the divine and mortal worlds, her story setting the stage for the birth of Romulus and Remus and the founding of Rome. Her narrative combines themes of usurpation, divine destiny, and the establishment of a new order – themes that are recurrent in the mythology surrounding the creation of the city of Rome.

Larunda

In Roman mythology, Larunda, also known as Lara or Lala, is a nymph with a unique and somewhat enigmatic background and role. She is most famous for her involvement in a story concerning Jupiter and her subsequent punishment, which led to her significant role in the Roman religious pantheon.

According to myth, Larunda was a beautiful nymph known for her loquacity and vivaciousness. Her story took a significant turn when she revealed Jupiter's affair with Juturna to Juno. Angered by her indiscretion, Jupiter cut out her tongue and ordered Mercury to escort her to the underworld. However, on the way, Mercury fell in love with her and fathered two children, the Lares, who became household spirits protecting home and hearth.

In the underworld, Larunda was transformed into a mute goddess, Muta or Tacita, and was venerated as a deity of the dead and silence. Her transformation and role in the underworld underscore the power and consequences of speech and secrets in Roman mythology. As a muted goddess, she represents the safeguarding of secrets and the respect for silence.

Virgil

Virgil, or Vergil, is not a mythical figure in Roman mythology but rather one of Rome's most renowned and celebrated poets. Born in 70 BCE near Mantua, in what is now modern Italy, Virgil's literary works have had a profound and lasting impact on Western literature and culture. He is best known for his epic poem, "The Aeneid," which has become a cornerstone of classical literature.

"The Aeneid" is a monumental work that tells the story of Aeneas, a Trojan who travels to Italy and becomes the ancestor of the Romans. This epic not only provides a mythical origin for Rome but also reflects and shapes Roman values, identity, and cultural ideals. Through Aeneas's journey, Virgil explores themes of duty, fate, and piety, aligning them with the Roman ideals of the time. The poem is also significant for its political undertones, as it was written during the turbulent period of Rome's transition from Republic to Empire, and it subtly comments on this transformation.

Virgil's other notable works include the "Georgics," a collection of poems celebrating the rural life and farming, and the "Eclogues" (or "Bucolics"), which are pastoral poems depicting the life of shepherds. These works are celebrated for their mastery of language and form, as well as their deep engagement with themes of nature, love, and social change.

Dido

In Roman mythology, Dido is a prominent figure known largely through Virgil's epic poem, "The Aeneid." She is the legendary founder and first queen of Carthage, a city on the coast of North Africa. Dido's story is one of love, sacrifice, and tragedy, and she plays a crucial role in the part of "The Aeneid" that deals with Aeneas's journey to Italy.

According to the myth, Dido fled from her homeland in the eastern Mediterranean to escape her brother Pygmalion. She arrived on the shores of North Africa, where she cleverly acquired a piece of land to establish Carthage, which would grow into a powerful and prosperous city. Dido is depicted as a strong, independent, and capable ruler, deeply loved by her people and dedicated to the welfare and success of her city.

Dido's fate takes a tragic turn when Aeneas, the Trojan hero journeying to found Rome, lands in Carthage. Dido and Aeneas fall in love, and for a time, Aeneas stays with her in Carthage. However, Aeneas is reminded by the gods of his destiny to found Rome and decides to leave Carthage, a decision that leads to Dido's despair. Feeling betrayed and abandoned, Dido commits suicide, uttering a curse that foreshadows the future enmity between Rome and Carthage.

Lavinia

In Roman mythology, Lavinia is a key figure prominently featured in Virgil's epic, "The Aeneid." She is the daughter of King Latinus and Queen Amata of the Latins, a tribe in Italy, and plays a crucial role in the latter part of the story. Lavinia is most famous for being the central figure in a love triangle involving Aeneas, the Trojan hero, and Turnus, the Rutulian prince, which ultimately leads to a war that shapes the destiny of Rome.

According to the myth, Lavinia was promised in marriage to Aeneas by her father, King Latinus, following an oracle's prophecy. However, this decision provokes the anger of Turnus, to whom Lavinia had been previously betrothed. The conflict over Lavinia's hand in marriage leads to a war between the Trojans and the Latins, with Aeneas ultimately emerging victorious.

Lavinia's role, while central to the plot of "The Aeneid," is primarily passive; she is a symbol around which the narrative unfolds rather than an active participant in the events. Her marriage to Aeneas is significant as it symbolizes the blending of Trojan and Latin blood, leading to the birth of the Roman people. Lavinia and Aeneas's union is seen as a foundational moment for the establishment and future greatness of Rome.

Laelaps

In Roman mythology, Laelaps is a legendary dog known for his incredible hunting ability. He was famed for his speed and was said to be a dog that could catch anything he hunted. Laelaps' story is intertwined with various myths and is often used to illustrate themes of predestination and the paradoxes arising from the clash of irresistible forces.

One of the most notable tales involving Laelaps is the story of his pursuit of the Teumessian Fox, a creature destined never to be caught. This tale presents a paradox: the dog who catches everything he hunts versus the fox who can never be caught. According to the myth, as Laelaps chased the Teumessian Fox, the chase seemed endless, with neither able to fulfill their destined roles. The paradox of this situation was resolved by Jupiter, who turned both creatures into stone, thus stopping the eternal chase.

Laelaps' mythological role extends beyond this specific story. He is often seen as a symbol of inevitability and the inescapable nature of fate. His participation in various myths reflects the Romans' fascination with and exploration of themes like destiny, the limitations of mortal abilities, and the intervention of the divine in resolving conflicts arising from fate and prophecy.

Cerberus

In Roman mythology, Cerberus is a formidable creature known as the guardian of the underworld. He is typically depicted as a massive, fearsome dog with multiple heads (usually three), tasked with guarding the entrance to the realm of the dead. Cerberus' role as the underworld's sentinel is to prevent the living from entering and the dead from leaving, ensuring the natural order of the passage between life and death is maintained.

Cerberus' fearsome reputation is matched by his physical description: in addition to his multiple heads, he is often portrayed with a serpent's tail and snakes protruding from various parts of his body, adding to his menacing presence. The multiple heads are said to symbolize his vigilance and ability to see in all directions, a necessary trait for the guardian of such an important threshold.

One of the most famous stories involving Cerberus in Roman mythology is his encounter with the hero Aeneas. In Virgil's "The Aeneid," Aeneas must enter the underworld as part of his journey. To pass Cerberus, Aeneas uses a soporific honey cake to calm and distract the beast, allowing him to move past the guardian safely and enter the realm of the dead.

Chimera

In Roman mythology, the Chimera is a fearsome, fire-breathing creature, notable for its hybrid appearance. It is typically described as having the body and head of a lion, with a goat's head rising from its back, and a serpent or dragon as its tail. This monstrous amalgamation makes the Chimera one of the more unique and terrifying creatures in Roman mythological lore.

The Chimera is often used as a symbol of the inexplicable and the monstrous, representing the fears and dangers that lie beyond the known world. Its fire-breathing ability adds to its formidable nature, making it a creature that is both awe-inspiring and terrifying. The Chimera's role in Roman mythology is primarily as an antagonist, a challenge to be overcome by heroes, demonstrating their bravery and prowess.

Sphinx

In Roman mythology, the Sphinx is a mythical creature with the body of a lion, the wings of a bird, and the face of a woman. This enigmatic being is renowned for its riddles and the mysterious nature of its challenges. The Sphinx in Roman culture, much like in other ancient mythologies, symbolizes the unknown and the mysterious, often serving as a guardian or a gatekeeper that poses questions or riddles to those who seek to pass.

Calydonian Boar

In Roman mythology, the Calydonian Boar is a formidable and monstrous creature that plays a central role in the story of the Calydonian Boar Hunt, a famous mythological event. This immense boar was known for its massive size, fearsome tusks, and destructive nature. According to the myth, the boar was sent by Diana, the goddess of the hunt, to ravage the land of Calydon as a form of retribution. The reason for Diana's anger varies in different versions of the story, but it often involves a slight or offense against her by the ruler of Calydon.

The devastation caused by the Calydonian Boar led to the assembly of a group of brave warriors and hunters from across the Roman world to hunt and kill the beast. This gathering included some of the most renowned figures of Roman mythology, making the Calydonian Boar Hunt a legendary event celebrated in Roman art and literature. The hunt itself was a dangerous and challenging endeavor, reflecting the themes of heroism, adventure, and the struggle against formidable foes.

CHAPTER 3:
CREATION MYTH

The Roman creation myth, much like the Greek one it was heavily influenced by, does not have a single, unified narrative describing the creation of the universe and life. Roman mythology largely adopted Greek gods and their myths, so the Roman creation story is similar to the Greek creation myth.

In Roman mythology, the universe was believed to have emerged from chaos, a primordial void or a formless, disordered state. From this chaos, the first gods and the elements were born.

In the beginning, there was nothing but an endless, formless void, a vast expanse of nothingness. This was Chaos, the primordial state of existence, where order and structure were concepts yet unborn, and time itself lingered in a perpetual slumber. It was a realm of infinite potential, a canvas untouched by the hands of creation.

As the eons passed in silent stillness, a change began to stir within the depths of Chaos. From the heart of this endless void, the first primordial entities emerged, not by design but by the inexplicable whims of the universe. These were not gods as we know them, but the very essence of elements and fundamental forces, raw and unbridled.

Among these primordial beings was Terra, the embodiment of Earth, a powerful and nurturing presence. She was the solidity in the midst of flux, a grounding force in the ever-shifting landscape of the void. Terra's emergence brought a sense of permanence to the chaos, a promise of something lasting and real.

Alongside Terra, other elemental forces came into being, shaping the nascent universe. There was Oceanus, the endless expanse of water, his form as fluid and unpredictable as the seas he represented. Then came the Air, a breath of life that whispered across the void, invisible yet ever-present. And deep within the bowels of Chaos, the Fire sparked into existence, a flickering dance of light and heat in the cold emptiness.

These primordial entities existed in a state of harmony, their natures complementary yet distinct. They were the first order in the universe, the foundational blocks upon which all else would be built. As they interacted, their energies mingled and coalesced, giving rise to new forms and possibilities.

It was from this divine interplay that the first gods were born, deities more akin to the ones of legend and lore. Among them was Saturn, a being of immense power and wisdom. He was the offspring of Terra and the Sky, inheriting the strength of the earth and the vastness of the heavens. Saturn's emergence marked a turning point in the cosmic saga, a shift towards a more structured and defined existence.

These early gods were different from the humans they would later create. They were colossal in size and power, their forms fluid and ever-changing, reflecting the dynamic nature of the universe they inhabited. They were the architects of reality, shaping the world through their will and desires.

As more gods and goddesses came into being, the chaos that had once reigned supreme began to recede. A new order was taking shape, a cosmos defined by rules and structures. The once formless void was being transformed, shaped into something tangible and real.

As the cosmos continued to evolve, the gods established their dominions, each carving out a realm within the burgeoning universe. Among these divine beings, Saturn rose to prominence.

Saturn's rule began in a time of great upheaval, as the early gods vied for control and influence. But it was Saturn, with his profound understanding of the cosmos and his formidable might, who emerged as the preeminent deity. He became the ruler of the gods, a king in a celestial court of immortals.

Under Saturn's reign, the Golden Age began. It was an era of peace and prosperity, a time when the harshness of existence was softened by the benevolence of the king of gods. Saturn ruled with a fair and even hand, his wisdom guiding the gods and shaping the destiny of the universe.

In this age, the world was a paradise, untouched by suffering or strife. The earth yielded its bounty without toil, the seasons changed in harmonious cycles, and mortals, should they have existed, would have known only joy and contentment. The gods themselves lived in a state of bliss, their days filled with feasts and merriment, their nights alight with the glow of starlit revelries.

However, this golden era was not to last. A prophecy whispered among the gods foretold the downfall of Saturn, a destiny that he could not escape. It was said that Saturn would be overthrown by one of his own children.

Fearing this prophecy, Saturn took drastic measures to protect his throne. Whenever Rhea bore him a child, he would swallow the newborn, imprisoning them within his own immortal form. In this way, he sought to prevent the prophecy from coming to pass, to maintain his rule and the Golden Age it had ushered in.

But fate, as always, finds a way. Rhea, Saturn's sister and wife, grieved for her lost children and yearned for a way to save her future offspring from Saturn's paranoia. When she was due to give birth to Jupiter, she devised a plan to save the child.

Rhea gave birth to Jupiter in secret, far from Saturn's watchful gaze. To deceive Saturn, she wrapped a stone in swaddling clothes and presented it to him as their newborn. Saturn, none the wiser, swallowed the stone, believing he had once again thwarted the prophecy.

Jupiter was hidden away, raised in secrecy, nurtured by the earth and sky, his heritage a blend of the terrestrial and the celestial. As he grew, so too did his power, and with it, the inevitability of the prophecy.

When the time was right, Jupiter challenged Saturn, confronting the king of gods in a battle that would determine the fate of the cosmos. The clash was titanic, a conflict that shook the very foundations of the universe. In the end, Jupiter emerged victorious, overthrowing Saturn and freeing his siblings from their father's grasp.

With Saturn's fall, the Golden Age came to an end. Jupiter ascended to the throne, ushering in a new era. He established a new order among the gods, reorganizing the divine hierarchy where the Dii Consentes now reigned supreme.

CHAPTER 4:
THE FOUNDING OF ROME

The story of Romulus and Remus is one of the most famous legends in Roman mythology, describing the founding of the city of Rome. It's a tale filled with intrigue, struggle, and divine intervention, illustrating the origins of Rome as a city destined for greatness.

In the kingdom of Alba Longa, ruled by the usurper King Amulius, a Vestal Virgin named Rhea Silvia lived in devoted service to the gods. Her beauty and grace caught the eye of Mars, the formidable god of war. From their union, under the cloak of secrecy and divine will, twins were conceived, a blend of mortal and divine, destined for greatness.

King Amulius, upon learning of the pregnancy, feared the prophecy that descendants of his royal line would overthrow him. In a desperate attempt to safeguard his throne, he ordered a cruel fate for the newborns: they were to be cast into the Tiber River, left to the whims of fate and the elements.

The infants, Romulus and Remus, swaddled and innocent, were set adrift on the river, their cradle a mere plaything of the currents. Yet, destiny had other plans. The river, as if recognizing the sanctity of its burden, gently carried the twins to safety, depositing them on the banks near the Palatine Hill, the future heart of Rome.

In this tranquil and wild place, their cries pierced the silence, an invocation to the gods. It was then that a remarkable savior appeared - a she-wolf, a creature of both fear and awe. Drawn by their cries, she approached the helpless infants with a demeanor that belied her fierce nature. In an act of unexpected tenderness, she lay down beside the twins, offering them her milk and warmth, nurturing them with a mother's care.

Their unusual cries eventually attracted the attention of a local shepherd named Faustulus. Upon discovering the twins with the she-wolf, Faustulus was struck by a sense of wonder and divine intervention. He took the boys to his home, where he and his wife, Acca Larentia, welcomed them into their humble abode.

In the shepherd's dwelling, Romulus and Remus found a new home. They grew under the watchful eyes of Faustulus and Acca Larentia, nurtured by the simplicity and honesty of pastoral life. The boys thrived, their heritage a hidden ember waiting to ignite. They were raised with the tales of gods and heroes, their minds filled with dreams of valor and their hearts with the stirrings of a destiny yet unknown.

As they matured, Romulus and Remus proved to be natural leaders, exuding charisma and strength. They became protectors of their flock, guardians of their community, often venturing into the wilderness, where they honed their skills in hunting and combat. Their actions spoke of a nobility that transcended their humble upbringing, a hint of the greatness that lay within them.

The story of their birth, shrouded in mystery and divine intrigue, was unknown to them until a fateful encounter set them on the path to their destiny. It was during a skirmish with the shepherds loyal to King Amulius that the twins were captured and brought before the king. In the royal courts of Alba Longa, their noble bearing and resemblance to the lineage of the deposed king, Numitor, did not go unnoticed.

Their grandfather, Numitor, upon seeing them, felt a stirring of recognition, a whisper of blood calling to blood. He pieced together their story, recognizing them as his daughter's sons, the children he thought lost to the river's depths. The revelation came like a lightning bolt, illuminating their past and igniting the flame of purpose in their hearts.

With the knowledge of their royal heritage, Romulus and Remus were no longer mere shepherds. They were princes, born to a legacy of power and responsibility. The injustice of Amulius's reign, the suffering of their mother Rhea Silvia, and the usurpation of their grandfather's throne boiled into a righteous fury within them.

Their anger and sense of justice galvanized the people of Alba Longa, who had long suffered under Amulius's tyranny. The twins became the focal point of a brewing rebellion, their cause a rallying cry for those who yearned for freedom and justice.

Romulus and Remus, with their newfound identity and the support of the people, led an uprising against King Amulius. The rebellion was a clash of not just arms but ideals, a fight for the soul of the kingdom. The brothers, skilled in combat and strategy, led their forces with a mix of cunning and bravery.

The battle for Alba Longa was fierce and fraught with peril. The streets echoed with the clash of swords, the cries of the warriors, and the determination of a people striving for liberation.

The climax of the struggle saw the fall of Amulius. The usurper king, defeated and disgraced, met his end, a poetic justice for the wrongs he had committed. With the tyrant's fall, the chains of oppression that had bound Alba Longa were shattered.

Romulus and Remus, having avenged their mother and restored their grandfather, Numitor, to the throne, were hailed as heroes. They had not only reclaimed their heritage but had also liberated their people from tyranny. Their victory was a testament to their courage, a sign of their fitness to rule.

In the aftermath of the rebellion, peace returned to Alba Longa. Numitor, once again king, sought to rebuild the kingdom, while Romulus and Remus, now aware of their potential and purpose, looked to the future.

The brothers, driven by a vision and a prophecy, contemplated a greater destiny. They dreamed of founding a new city, one that would stand as a testament to their journey and a beacon of hope and power. The land by the Tiber, where they had been nurtured by the she-wolf, called to them, its destiny intertwined with theirs. It was more than a place; it was a symbol of their survival, a land imbued with destiny. Here, they resolved to establish a city, a testament to their journey and a sanctuary for the future.

However, the shared dream soon led to a bitter dispute. Each brother favored a different hill for the site of the new city: Romulus preferred the Palatine Hill, the site of their salvation by the she-wolf, while Remus argued for the Aventine Hill, with its strategic advantages. The decision of where to build was not merely a matter of preference but of vision and destiny.

To resolve their impasse, the brothers turned to the ancient practice of augury – interpreting the will of the gods through the flight of birds. Each brother took a position on his chosen hill, watching the skies for divine signs. Remus saw six vultures flying, but Romulus saw twelve. This difference sparked a heated argument, as each claimed the gods' favor and the right to name and found the new city.

The dispute escalated, the tension between the brothers mirroring the unsettled sky above. In a moment of anger, fueled by the passion of their visions and the weight of destiny, Romulus struck Remus. The blow was fatal, a tragic end to the bond that had carried them through so much. Remus lay slain, a casualty of the very dream he had helped to conceive.

With heavy heart, Romulus proceeded with the founding of the city. He solemnly marked the boundaries of Rome on the Palatine Hill, declaring it a refuge for the exiled, the homeless, and the ambitious. The city was named Rome, after Romulus himself, a lasting reminder of its founder and the price paid for its birth.

As the first king of Rome, Romulus laid the foundations of a city that was destined for greatness. He established its institutions, its laws, and its legions, imbuing it with strength, order, and a sense of destiny. Under his rule, Rome grew rapidly, attracting people from far and wide, becoming a melting pot of cultures, ideas, and aspirations.

CHAPTER 5: THE RAPE OF THE SABINE WOMEN

The story of the Rape of the Sabine Women is a famous episode in Roman mythology that illustrates the early history of Rome. This event is traditionally dated to around 750-752 BC and centers on the first generation of Roman citizens.

According to the legend, after founding Rome, Romulus, the city's first king, faced a significant problem: a severe shortage of women among his citizens. To secure the future of his new city, Romulus needed to find wives for his predominantly male followers. However, neighboring communities were unwilling to provide their daughters in marriage to the Romans due to ongoing conflicts and mistrust.

To overcome this obstacle, Romulus devised a plan. He organized a grand festival and invited neighboring Sabine people, including their families, to attend the festivities. The Sabines, unaware of the Romans' intentions, attended the event with their families, including many young women.

During the festival, at a prearranged signal, the Roman men seized the Sabine women and carried them off. This act of abduction is referred to as the "Rape of the Sabine Women." The term "rape" in this context comes from the Latin word "rapio," meaning "to seize" or "to carry off," and does not necessarily imply sexual assault as understood in modern terms.

The immediate aftermath of the abduction was marked by outrage and indignation among the Sabines and their allies. The Sabine king, Titus Tatius, was particularly incensed by this act of treachery and began to mobilize for war. The Sabines, along with their allies who shared grievances against Rome, prepared for a retaliatory strike. Before the main conflict with the Sabines erupted, Romulus, the founder and king of Rome, faced and overcame challenges from other neighboring tribes, consolidating his power and preparing for the inevitable confrontation with the Sabines.

The war with the Sabines was both intense and pivotal. The Sabines, a strong and well-organized force under the command of Titus Tatius, posed a significant threat to the young Roman state. The climax of this conflict was a fierce battle in the Roman Forum, the center of Romulus' burgeoning city. This battle was not just a fight for supremacy but also a struggle for the very heart and future of Rome.

Amidst this chaos and bloodshed, a remarkable event occurred that shifted the course of the conflict. The Sabine women, who had been seized by the Romans and had since integrated into Roman society as wives and mothers, intervened in a dramatic and emotional plea for peace. Braving the dangers of the battlefield, they placed themselves between the clashing armies of their fathers and their husbands, beseeching both sides to spare the blood of their kin. Their actions underscored the tragic reality that any further violence would only lead to the devastation of their own families on both sides.

Their intervention struck a chord with both the Romans and the Sabines. Moved by the bravery and words of these women, the two sides ceased hostilities. This moment of compassion and understanding led to a peace treaty and an agreement for joint rule between Romulus and Titus Tatius. The resolution of the conflict brought about a merging of Roman and Sabine cultures, enriching the Roman state both culturally and socially.

The legend of the Rape of the Sabine Women, culminating in the peace forged by the women themselves, became emblematic of the power of reconciliation and unity. It highlighted the role of wisdom and empathy in resolving conflicts and stood as a testament to Rome's ability to assimilate and harmonize diverse peoples and cultures, a characteristic that would define much of its subsequent history.

CHAPTER 6:
THE CALYDONIAN BOAR HUNT

E nter chapter... In the rich tapestry of Roman mythology, the story of the Calydonian Boar Hunt stands out as a captivating blend of divine retribution, human valor, and tragic consequence. This legend, set in the verdant landscapes of ancient Calydon, weaves a narrative that reflects the deeply intertwined relationships between gods and mortals in Roman lore.

The saga begins with King Oeneus of Calydon, a ruler blessed with a prosperous and fertile kingdom. During a year of particularly abundant harvest, Oeneus, in a ceremonial gesture of gratitude, made lavish offerings to the Roman deities to honor their contributions to his land's fertility and success. However, in his devotions, he overlooked Diana, the esteemed goddess of the hunt and the wilderness. Diana, known for her swift retribution and fierce temperament, took great offense at this oversight. In response, she summoned a monstrous boar of colossal size and strength, unleashing it upon the lands of Calydon. This boar was no mere animal; it was a creature of divine wrath, tearing through the countryside, ravaging crops, and instilling fear among the people with its fiery eyes and razor-sharp tusks.

Faced with this menace, King Oeneus realized that extraordinary measures were needed. He summoned heroes from across the land to partake in what was to be a grand hunt, promising glory and honor to those who would help rid his kingdom of the boar. Among those who answered this call was Meleager, the prince of Calydon and a warrior of remarkable prowess. Meleager's participation in the hunt would prove to be both pivotal and tragic in the unfolding of events.

As the hunters gathered, one figure stood out: Atalanta, a woman of exceptional skill in the art of hunting. Her presence in the hunt, unusual and controversial due to her gender, became a focal point of the story. Atalanta was not merely a participant; she was a symbol of grace, strength, and the breaking of conventions in a world dominated by male heroes. Meleager, captivated by her skill and spirit, championed her involvement, setting the stage for a complex interplay of admiration, rivalry, and eventual tragedy.

The hunt for the Calydonian Boar was a perilous endeavor, filled with danger at every turn. The boar, a beast of Diana's wrath, was a formidable opponent, charging with lethal force and evading the attacks of the hunters with terrifying agility. The heroes, despite their valor and strength, found themselves repeatedly thwarted by the creature's might.

The turning point in the hunt came when Atalanta, demonstrating her unparalleled skill, succeeded in drawing the first blood from the boar. Her arrow, guided by a blend of divine favor and human determination, struck the boar, slowing its rampage. Inspired and driven by Atalanta's success, Meleager then delivered the final, fatal blow to the beast, ending its reign of terror over Calydon.

The aftermath of the hunt, however, was far from celebratory. Meleager, in a gesture of admiration and affection, awarded the hide of the boar to Atalanta, igniting a fierce dispute among the hunters. This act of honor towards Atalanta was perceived as a slight by some, particularly Meleager's uncles. The ensuing quarrel escalated into violence, with Meleager killing his uncles in a fit of rage.

The tragic spiral continued as Meleager's mother, Althaea, consumed by grief and anger at the death of her brothers, sought revenge against her own son.

At Meleager's birth, the Fates, who in Roman mythology are the personifications of destiny, appeared and prophesied that Meleager would live only as long as a certain piece of wood, then burning in the fireplace, remained unconsumed. Althaea, upon hearing this prophecy, quickly extinguished the fire and preserved the piece of wood, thereby securing her son's life as long as the wood remained safe.

However, in the aftermath of the Calydonian Boar Hunt and the subsequent killing of her brothers, Althaea was torn between her love for her son and her duty to avenge her brothers. In a moment of overwhelming anguish and a sense of justice, she decided to carry out the terms of the Fates' prophecy. Althaea retrieved the piece of wood that she had saved years ago and threw it into the fire. As the wood was consumed by the flames, the life of Meleager was inextricably bound to its fate.

Meleager, far from the scene and unaware of his mother's actions, suddenly felt his life force ebbing away. As the wood turned to ash, Meleager's life was extinguished, fulfilling the prophecy of the Fates. His death marked a tragic end to the hero who had valiantly defeated the Calydonian Boar but could not escape the inexorable decrees of destiny.

CHAPTER 7: THE MYTH OF VERTUMNUS AND POMONA

The myth of Vertumnus and Pomona is a charming and romantic tale from Roman mythology, focusing on themes of love, transformation, and persuasion. This story stands out for its focus on more gentle and cunning aspects of love, rather than the grand, epic narratives often found in Roman myths.

Pomona was a nymph and the goddess of fruit trees, gardens, and orchards. She was renowned for her skill in horticulture and was deeply devoted to the care of her plants. Pomona had her own orchard which she tended with great dedication and skill, creating a paradise of fruit-laden trees and blossoming plants. She was beautiful and admired by many, but Pomona had little interest in the advances of potential suitors, preferring the company of her beloved trees and gardens.

Vertumnus, the god of seasons, change, and plant growth, became enamored with Pomona. Vertumnus, known for his power to change his form at will, was captivated not only by Pomona's beauty but also by her dedication to her orchard. He longed to win her heart but knew that she was indifferent to the usual courtship rituals.

In his quest to gain Pomona's affection, Vertumnus employed his unique ability to transform himself. He took on multiple disguises to enter Pomona's orchard, hoping to get close to her and win her over. He appeared in various guises, such as a reaper, a fisherman, and a peasant, among others, each time attempting to engage Pomona in conversation and pique her interest. Despite his efforts, Pomona remained oblivious to his advances, dedicated solely to her orchard.

Finally, Vertumnus decided to try a different approach. He took on the form of an old woman, a wise and gentle figure, and entered the orchard once more. As an elderly woman, Vertumnus offered Pomona advice on love and marriage, praising the virtues of Vertumnus himself and telling her of his genuine love and admiration for her. During this conversation, he cleverly wove in praise for the harmony between the natural world and love, suggesting that Pomona's dedication to her orchard could be complemented by a partnership with someone who shared her values.

As the conversation flowed, Pomona found herself drawn to the tales and insights shared by the 'old woman'. There was an earnestness and a sincerity in the words that resonated with her, stirring emotions that she had long set aside in favor of her beloved gardens. It was then, amidst the verdant surroundings teeming with life and under the gentle gaze of the being she knew as an elderly matron, that the moment of revelation arrived.

Vertumnus, sensing a shift in Pomona's heart and feeling the time was ripe, decided to unveil his true identity. The air seemed to still for a moment as the magical transformation began. The guise of the old woman melted away, like morning mist under the touch of the sun. In its place, the true form of Vertumnus emerged, revealing a handsome and vibrant god, the embodiment of the changing seasons. His eyes, reflecting a depth of genuine love and admiration, met Pomona's in a tender gaze, bridging the distance between them.

The orchard itself seemed to respond to this revelation, with the leaves rustling softly as if in approval, and the fruits appearing to ripen and glow more richly in the presence of their patron deity. Vertumnus stood before Pomona, not with the arrogance of a god assured of his divine right, but with the vulnerability of one who has laid bare his heart, awaiting judgment.

Pomona, taken aback by the transformation, gazed upon Vertumnus. The realization dawned on her that the love and admiration he had professed were sincere. In Vertumnus, she saw not just another suitor, but a kindred spirit, one who understood and shared her love for the natural world. His persistence, the respect he had shown in his approach, and his ability to appreciate the essence of her being, all these spoke to Pomona's heart.

The revelation of Vertumnus's true form marked the end of his pursuit and the beginning of a new chapter. Pomona's initial surprise gave way to admiration and then to love. In Vertumnus, she found a companion, a lover, and a co-guardian of the natural world.

CHAPTER 8:
HERCULES AND CACUS

The story of Hercules and Cacus is a tale from Roman mythology that highlights the heroism of Hercules (known as Heracles in Greek mythology) and his encounter with the monstrous figure Cacus. This myth is particularly significant in Roman culture as it integrates the renowned Greek hero Hercules into the fabric of Roman mythological and cultural heritage.

Hercules, during his famous Twelve Labors, arrived in the region that would later become Rome. He was driving the cattle he had obtained as part of his tenth labor - the task of stealing the cattle of the monster Geryon. As Hercules rested near the River Tiber, Cacus, a fearsome and monstrous creature, saw the magnificent herd. Cacus was a giant, known for his terrifying presence and for living in a cave on the Aventine Hill. He was the son of Vulcan, the god of fire, and had a penchant for terrorizing the local populace.

Intrigued by the cattle, Cacus decided to steal them. He took a number of the herd, dragging them by their tails to his cave so that their tracks would not give away the direction they were taken. He hid the cattle in his cave, a place so deep and labyrinthine that finding anything within it was nearly impossible.

When Hercules awoke, he noticed that some of his cattle were missing. He began a search but was initially baffled by the lack of tracks. Eventually, the remaining cattle began to stir as they passed by Cacus's cave, and the stolen cattle responded from inside the cave. This alerted Hercules to the location of his missing herd.

Enraged by the theft, Hercules approached the cave. Cacus, realizing that Hercules had discovered his theft, tried to block the entrance by rolling a massive stone across it. Undeterred, Hercules smashed his way through the rock barrier with his immense strength.

A fierce battle ensued between Hercules and Cacus. Cacus, able to breathe fire, was a formidable opponent. However, Hercules, known for his incredible strength and heroic combat skills, ultimately overcame the monster. The fight ended with Hercules strangling Cacus or clubbing him to death, depending on the version of the story.

The defeat of Cacus by Hercules was celebrated by the local people, who were relieved to be rid of the terror that Cacus had long inflicted upon them. It was also said that this event led to the founding of a great altar, the Ara Maxima, by Evander, a figure from Greek mythology who had migrated to Italy.

The story of Hercules and Cacus not only highlights the valor and strength of Hercules but also serves as a foundational myth for the city of Rome. It symbolizes the triumph of civilization and order over barbarism and chaos, a theme common in many Roman myths.

CHAPTER 9:
JUPITER AND THE BEE

In Roman mythology, the tale of Jupiter and the Bee is a poignant fable that encapsulates themes of ambition, pride, and the unintended consequences of one's desires. This story, while simple in its structure, conveys deep moral lessons that were highly regarded in Roman society.

The narrative begins with a bee, a creature skilled in the art of making honey. This bee was not just any ordinary bee; she was extraordinarily proud of her ability to produce honey, a substance revered for its sweetness and purity. Her pride in her craft and her creation led her to conceive a bold plan: to present her honey to Jupiter, the king of the gods, and seek a special favor in return.

With a sample of her finest honey, the bee embarked on a journey to Mount Olympus, the majestic and formidable home of the Roman gods. Upon reaching the divine abode, she presented her gift to Jupiter. The god, known for his might and sovereignty over both gods and mortals, was pleasantly surprised by the quality of the honey. Impressed by its exquisite taste, he graciously commended the bee for her skillful work.

In response to the bee's exceptional gift, Jupiter, in a gesture of divine generosity, offered to grant the bee any wish she desired. The bee, emboldened by Jupiter's offer and driven by her pride, requested a boon that she believed would elevate her status and protect her precious creation. She asked for the power to sting, a weapon to guard her honey against those who would dare to steal it.

Jupiter, however, perceived the deeper implications of such a gift. He recognized the bee's ambition and the potential harm that such power could inflict. Thus, while agreeing to grant her request, he imposed a significant limitation. He bestowed upon the bee the ability to sting, but with a grave condition: the use of her sting would be a sacrificial act, as it would lead to her own death. The sting, once used, would remain in the victim's flesh and consequently tear away from the bee's body, bringing about her demise.

This condition imposed by Jupiter was a lesson in humility and foresight. It served as a warning against the dangers of overreaching and the importance of understanding the weight of one's actions. The bee, in her quest to protect her honey, gained the means to defend it but at the ultimate cost – her life would be forfeit upon using this defense.

The story of Jupiter and the Bee, thus, resonates as a moral tale within Roman mythology, emphasizing the delicate balance between ambition and prudence. It reflects the Roman values of wisdom, humility, and the recognition of the potential consequences of one's actions, while also explaining why bees have the ability to sting!

CONCLUSION

As we draw the curtains on this journey through the enchanting and complex realm of Roman mythology, we are left with a tapestry rich in narrative depth, moral lessons, and cultural insights. The myths recounted in this collection are more than just tales of gods, heroes, and fantastical creatures; they are the echoes of an ancient civilization's soul, offering us timeless reflections on human nature and the world around us.

The gods and goddesses, with their grandeur and flaws, mirror the range of human emotions and experiences, from the heights of love and compassion to the depths of jealousy and vengeance. The stories of demi-gods, heroes, nymphs, and mortals invite us to contemplate the interplay between the divine and the mundane, highlighting the indomitable spirit of humanity in the face of overwhelming odds.

In the Roman Creation Myth and the legendary founding of Rome, we find the seeds of Rome's identity, a blend of divine providence and human ambition that would shape the empire's destiny. The tale of the Rape of the Sabine Women, with its themes of conflict and reconciliation, reflects the complexities of societal integration and the formation of communities.

The Calydonian Boar Hunt and the story of Hercules and Cacus present a world where heroism and moral dilemmas coexist, reminding us of the perennial struggle between right and wrong, strength and wisdom. The myth of Vertumnus and Pomona offers a respite with its tender narrative of love and transformation, revealing the softer side of Roman mythology.

Finally, the fable of Jupiter and the Bee leaves us with a profound moral lesson about ambition and the importance of considering the consequences of our desires, a theme that resonates through many of the myths we have explored.

In these stories, we find not only the foundations of Roman culture and religion but also universal themes that continue to resonate with us today. They remind us of our connection to the past and the shared human quest for understanding, meaning, and connection in an ever-changing world.

I hope you have enjoyed this exploration into the world of Roman Mythology. If you would like to share your feedback, it is greatly appreciated if you could take a minute to leave us a review on Amazon. It really helps us to continue producing books that readers love!

And finally, if you liked this book, please keep an eye out for the other books in this series, also available for sale on Amazon as well as through many other online retailers. The other books in this series include:

- Greek Mythology: A Collection of the Best Greek Myths

- Norse Mythology: A Collection of the Best Norse Myths

- Egyptian Mythology: A Collection of the Best Egyptian Myths

- Celtic Mythology: A Collection of the Best Celtic Myths

www.ingramcontent.com/pod-product-compliance
Lightning Source LLC
Chambersburg PA
CBHW071026120626
46546CB00003B/1228